CONTAINERS
— AND —
BASKETS
— FOR —
YEAR ROUND
COLOUR

CONTAINERS
— AND —
BASKETS
— FOR —
YEAR ROUND
COLOUR

Peter McHoy

WARD LOCK

ACKNOWLEDGEMENTS

The publishers are grateful to the following for granting permission to reproduce the colour photographs:

Peter McHoy (Cover: left-hand photograph; pp. 7, 10, 23, 27, 35, 46, 47, 51, 58, 71, 79, 82, 83, 86, 103, 110, 115, 118 and 119); Photos Horticultural Picture Library (pp. 2, 15, 18, 19, 30, 38, 43, 54, 74, 94 and 114); Harry Smith Horticultural Photographic Collection (Cover: right-hand photograph; pp. 11, 14, 59, 63, 67, 95 and 126); Elizabeth Whiting & Associates (Cover: main photograph); and Pat Brindley (p. 91).

All the line drawings were drawn by Mike Shoebridge

First published in Great Britain in 1993
by Ward Lock Limited, Villiers House, 41/47 Strand,
London WC2N 5JE, England
A Cassell Imprint

Text filmset by Chapterhouse, Formby, L37 3PX

Printed and bound in Hong Kong
by
Dah Hua Printing Co. Ltd.

CIP data for this book is available upon application
from The British Library

ISBN 0 7063 7099 6

CONTENTS

PREFACE

CONTAINER GARDENING SHOULD be much more than a mere means of adding a touch of colour to the summer patio or even bringing a welcome to the front door with a hanging basket: it should be a year round hobby in its own right, like growing alpines, greenhouse gardening, or collecting bonsai.

If container gardening has failed to inspire you as a year round hobby, either for lack of inspiration or because a few failures have dampened your enthusiasm, this book should make you want to take up container gardening with renewed optimism. It aims to show you how to make the most of containers in all seasons, so that you can enjoy this richly rewarding form of gardening throughout the year. The first four chapters are arranged by seasons. Summer is the zenith of the container gardening year, and the time when you can be most adventurous and flamboyant with your choice of plants, and many of the seasonal planting suggestions are inevitably devoted to this period. But make the most of your containers by replanting them to extend the season . . . there are plenty of suggestions in the appropriate chapters.

Constant replanting of tubs and troughs is not everyone's idea of entertainment and perennials that can be left to grow and improve each year, perhaps brightened up from time to time with a few additional seasonal plants, can be just as striking. The effect is often more subtle than bright bedding plants, but this may be just the impression that you want to create in a cool courtyard garden or as a focal point in a leafy or formally elegant part of the garden. The chapter on Permanent Plantings will give you lots of ideas to try.

Choosing the plants is part of the fun of container gardening, and creating planting plans is one of the pleasures of winter when there is not a lot that you can do in the garden. The plant profiles in Chapter 9 include most of the plants mentioned in the planting suggestions, but space rather than ideas is as limiting in a book of this size as in the garden itself. Many good summer container plants have been left out to make space for those that will help to extend container gardening into a year-round activity. The list is no more than a cross-section of good container plants, and it leaves plenty of scope for the adventurous to try others.

Containers do not have to be mere receptacles for plants. Many are ornamental enough to make a contribution in their own right. Good container gardening is about more than growing plants successfully, it is about using the containers

*Mixed baskets are popular, but choose plants well-balanced in vigour. This one contains petunias, lobelia and black-eyed Susan (*Thunbergia alata*).*

creatively as part of garden design. Chapter 7, Creative with Containers, shows how the choice of containers, and where and how you position them, also contributes to the success of a well-planned container garden.

Neither containers nor plants are any guarantee of success. Know-how and good growing techniques are nowhere more important than with growing plants in containers. In this unnatural environment, where the soil dries out rapidly and plants are often packed into a relatively tiny amount of compost, jobs like watering and feeding assume an importance far above that for the rest of the garden. How you plant, what you plant in, and the diligence with which you look after them afterwards, are far more important than the choice of plants. The best plants will be disappointing if you neglect them. Chapter 8, Know-how, is packed with tips to make light of the chores while being heavy on practical advice to help you grow really superb container plants.

If you are new to container gardening, you may like to read up on ideas for containers themselves first of all – there are plenty of ideas in Chapter 7. But the heart of gardening is, after all, the plants themselves, so the first four chapters look at the seasons in turn – from the excitement of the first flowers of spring to the challenge of winter.

P.McH.

CHAPTER 1

SPRING DISPLAYS

SPRING SHOULD EXPLODE suddenly into a multi-coloured volcano of colour. There is nothing subtle about spring: for months bulbs and biennials make painfully slow progress, then suddenly within a matter of days buds appear and open and the dull days (though not necessarily the sharp frosts and biting winds) of winter are over. The colours are often bright and garish too, with bright yellows and vivid reds dominating the more subtle shades. Your containers, too, should celebrate the end of winter, with bright and bold displays in tubs, windowboxes, and wall baskets. Be prepared to spend money on a bold display of bright bulbs to start the year with a bang, but do not overlook early border perennials that can also make a bright splash of colour . . . often for less cost and with more reliable year-on-year display.

USING BULBS

Bulbs are almost synonymous with spring, but they are not without problems, especially in containers. To avoid disappointment choose kinds that will put on a good show the first season. Some, such as winter aconites and snowdrops, need a few years to settle down before they look really impressive, and these work best in permanent plantings. Others, such as *Iris reticulata* and *I. danfordiae*, and many tulips put on a good display the first season then tend to split up into many smaller bulbs that take several years to reach flowering size, so the subsequent display can be very patchy and unpredictable – something acceptable in the open ground but not in a container where gaps are not only disappointing but highly conspicuous.

With few exceptions, bulbs for containers should be the top-flowering size, and preferably bought afresh from a reputable supplier each autumn; otherwise they should be reliable regular flowerers, once established, and planted as part of a permanent container. Buying fresh daffodils and tulips for your containers each year is not an extravagance as they can be planted in beds and borders afterwards, where they will give pleasure for many more years.

It is necessary to choose suitable varieties as well as the right kinds of bulbs. Tall daffodils that sway enticingly in the wind on long stalks may look pretty naturalized in an area of grass, but in a windowbox where they receive the rebound of turbulent air as it hits the wall, they simply bend and break unless you support them with canes – which hardly enhances their beauty. Dwarf varieties have as much impact as large ones in the smaller perspective of a windowbox, with none of the drawbacks of the larger varieties. Tall lily-flowered tulips will grace flower beds with a touch of elegance and style, especially if they are interplanted with bushy low-growing plants such as forget-me-nots, but they are only suitable for containers like large tubs and half-barrels on the patio, where their proportions are right and they are less exposed to the ravaging effect of the wind. Select compact types such as early double tulips or some of the species hybrids for a windowbox.

Spring-flowering bulbs have a major weakness as container plants: their flowering season is often brief. Overcome this shortcoming by interplanting with spring bedding plants such as double daisies and pansies to extend the season, but remember to 'balance' the plants: there is little point in planting pansies with tall varieties of daffodils as the effect will simply look a mess after the bulbs have flowered and the daffodil foliage submerges the smaller plants until it dies back.

It is tempting to plant different varieties of the same kind of bulb for succession of bloom (by planting various varieties of hyacinths it is possible to have them in bloom over a month or more), but who wants a handful of blooms among a collection of tight buds and dead or dying flowers? For real impact, plant for a mass of colour, even if this is short-lived. If you want to extend the season, plant up some additional pots of later-flowering bulbs to replace the earlier ones as these fade.

PLANT CLOSE

A common mistake is to plant bulbs too far apart. Fairly wide spacing is acceptable in beds and borders where they can be left to multiply to form established clumps. Container displays are usually one-offs, and even those bulbs that do flower reliably the second year are generally planted elsewhere to make way for summer flowers. To achieve the kind of dense flowering clumps that you find in the garden or see in illustrations in bulb catalogues, plant the bulbs almost touching. Plants like crocuses will then look as though they are growing in a floriferous clump and will not appear to be a collection of single plants, spaced soldier-like.

This makes planting bulbs expensive, but you will almost certainly be better pleased with one container really well planted than three sparse ones that lack impact.

SPRING BEDDING

Plants normally used for spring bedding, such as double daisies, forget-me-nots, pansies, polyanthus, primroses and wallflowers, all make good container plants.

Tulipa praestans 'Fusilier' makes a particularly good show because it has multiple flower heads. The shallow container makes this a well-proportioned display.

Use them to extend the period of interest where bulbs are used, and to fill in around the base of taller bulbs (they will provide a degree of hidden support in windy conditions.)

Provided you choose varieties that are tough and hardy, choice is largely a matter of personal preference and the colour effect that you want to create. With the exception of forget-me-nots, most garden centres sell spring bedding plants in mixed colours, but for really clever colour blending with other flowers it is best to choose single colours so that you can control the effect. Good nurseries sometimes sell single-colour selections, otherwise you will have to grow your own from seed.

Wallflowers need special thought. Because they are so deliciously fragrant it is tempting to place them in tubs or troughs by the front door or in the porch, but in poor light they grow tall and drawn and seldom live up to expectations. Grow them in an open position, or at least where the light is good, and be sure to choose a dwarf variety for a windowbox.

Siberian wallflowers are less popular, but they make a marvellous pool of gold or pale yellow planted *en masse* in a shallow dish-shaped container.

Opposite: *Winter-flowering pansies are often at their best in spring. They are easy and inexpensive to raise yourself and can be depended upon for a bold splash of early colour. In this half-basket a few clumps of aubrieta add a touch of extra interest.*

WINDOWBOXES

Yellow daffodils dominate the spring scene, and the colour is reflected in the yellow of primroses, polyanthus and many tulips. Let this bright and cheerful colour bring a ray of light to a sunless side of the house (if the light is really poor, grow them in good light until they are just coming into flower then move the boxes into position). Use yellows to enhance blue flowers that often look a little 'heavy' on their own.

Sunny yellows and bright blues

Create a charming 'natural-looking' windowbox with primroses (*Primula vulgaris*), but do not dig up wild ones – they are easily raised from seed readily available from seedsmen if you can't find a nursery or garden centre that sells them. If the plants are large and well-established you will need only two or three for a 60 cm (2 ft) windowbox. For a 'wild' and informal appearance, avoid the multicoloured hybrid primroses that are widely available. These lack the delicate charm of the wild type and unless very carefully hardened off can be disappointing outdoors. Interplant the primroses with the blue *Scilla siberica*, which are about the same height and should open their delicate, brilliant blue bells at the same time.

The primroses have a long flowering period and can be planted in the garden when you need the boxes for summer plants. Scillas also move well, but flowering the second year may be patchy, so naturalize them where they can multiply undisturbed.

These low-growing plants lack height, so if you want something taller you could try bluebells instead of scillas, which will give your windowbox a native woodland feel. Bluebells (which you can buy from bulb merchants) can look a bit sparse the first year, but grape hyacinths (*Muscari armeniacum*) are totally dependable (they will also multiply and flower freely in the garden afterwards). They tend to look stiff and formal in comparison with the scillas, however, which have a dainty charm that lets them merge unobtrusively and harmoniously with the primroses.

Daffodils and hyacinths

For a more formal blue and yellow colour scheme, daffodils and hyacinths make a happy marriage. Choose dwarf, early daffodils such as 'February Gold' to plant along the back of the box, and use a blue hyacinth such as the navy 'Ostara'. There is a degree of luck in getting the timing right, but if flowering is not perfectly synchronized you will have the benefit of a prolonged flowering period. In a large box, try planting a couple of varieties of hyacinths for succession, so that one of them coincides with the daffodils and the others extend the period of interest. For an early blue, plant 'Ostara', with 'Delft Blue' to follow on.

Blue grape hyacinths and yellow multi-headed *Narcissus triandrus* hybrids and varieties such as 'Hawera' complement each other admirably in a slightly later display.

Ways with irises

A collection of yellow and blue dwarf irises is also very striking, but plant in clumps rather than rows. The yellow *Iris danfordiae* and blue *Iris reticulata* and its varieties look harmonious, and add a little height with a miniature daffodil such as 'Tête-à-Tête' at the back, which will blend with the yellow irises. *Iris danfordiae* often flowers earlier than the blue irises if you plant them together, but the daffodils will maintain the colour contrast if this happens.

All these plants are often sold in pots in garden centres in spring, so there is an ideal opportunity to make an 'instant' windowbox if you forgot to plant in the autumn. Buy them in bud so that you know they will flower together, and keep them in the tight clumps when you plant (simply plunge the pots in the compost, or knock them out and plant together as a root-ball).

Perfect pansies

Pansies are perfect windowbox plants. They are small and compact, flower for a long time, and are easier to deadhead and maintain in vigorous growth than when planted in beds or borders. The 'Universal' range is sold as 'winter-flowering' but they really only bloom prolifically in spring. They are usually sold in garden centres with one or two blooms already open, so mix and match the colours, such as lemon or white with rich blue, or gold with velvety mahogany to give the best effect. Colour combinations give pansy-only windowboxes real charm, and clever colour co-ordination helps to offset the risk of monotony created by an even height.

Alpine boxes

Alpine windowboxes can be a year-round feature (see page 62), especially if plenty of evergreens are chosen, but plant a box with free-flowering and vigorous alpines in the autumn to produce a respectable and colourful show in spring. You may prefer to keep the plants in pots, simply plunged into the windowbox soil, to make planting out in the garden easier when you want to use the container for summer bedding, but a more convincing planting effect can be achieved if they are knocked out of their pots and 'landscaped' so that some trail over the edge, while others jostle with small pieces of strategically placed rock – and of course a dressing of stone chippings will finish it off and make the box more presentable in the winter while the plants are just ticking over.

For this kind of spring alpine windowbox, go for the bright and cheerful even if they are rampant, rather than the more restrained alpines suitable for a permanently planted container. *Alyssum saxatile* is a good choice where you want something to trail over the edge, as even young plants will make an impressive carpet of small gold flowers. Arabis is a cheap and cheerful plant and the common white one is a good companion for the blues and mauves of aubrieta, but try a variegated form such as *A. ferdinandi-coburgii* 'Variegata' (cushions of evergreen white and green foliage) or 'Old Gold' (gold and green) to provide some winter interest as well as white flowers in spring.

Rock phlox, such as *P. douglasii* and *P. subulata*, are also reliable and there are

You do not need a lot of bulbs for a striking display if you can mix them with other spring bedding plants. Here yellow tulips have been underplanted with a compact variety of yellow wallflowers, and blue pansies add contrast.

plenty of varieties in shades of blue, pink, red, and white. Small plants can be disappointing the first year, however, so pay a bit more and plant large ones with an extra year's growth.

Saxifrages are useful because most of them contribute a carpet of attractive rosettes of foliage as well as delicate flowers in shades of pink, yellow and white. These are not good long-term companions for rampant plants like aubrieta and arabis, but they can be used together for a one-off display before being planted in the garden.

BASKETS

Baskets left outdoors all winter seldom do well. Being exposed on all sides the compost becomes frozen solid for long periods and even really tough plants like ivies can look sad by the time spring arrives. Plant up your spring basket in the autumn but keep it in a cool or cold greenhouse, even a cold frame, then hang it out in spring after careful hardening off if necessary. You do not need to hang the basket during the winter, just stand it on a bucket or large flower pot to make it stable.

Opposite: *Spring-flowering perennials such as aubrieta and this yellow* Alyssum montanum *are useful for containers that can be left permanently planted. In this container, made from old tyres, the white tulips will be replaced by bedding plants in early summer.*

Pansy balls

Plant winter-flowering pansies around the sides and in the top of the basket, but remove any early flowers that appear during mild spells in the winter so that the plants become bushy. By spring, when you can let them start flowering, the pansies should have grown enough to make a ball-like display. For a true ball of flowers, however, you must be able to hang the basket during the winter (perhaps in a cold greenhouse) so that you can plant right down to the base.

Crocus colour

Crocus corms can be planted around the sides of a basket, but line it with moss so that the shoots can easily grow through. Put them in layer by layer as you fill the basket with compost, but plant plenty of them – they look unconvincing with just a few flowers here and there. Plant a mixture of early *Crocus chrysanthus* varieties and later large-flowered Dutch crocuses to extend what would otherwise be a brief show. Some crocuses can be planted in the top too, but include something bushy like pansies, polyanthus or forget-me-nots that will spread the flowering period and create a more rounded effect.

Miniature bulbs

The choice of small bulbs for hanging pots and baskets with solid sides is limited only by your imagination, but bear in mind that small bulbs are often not very visible when viewed from below. Those that spread and cascade are more successful than rather stiff and upright bulbs.

If you want bulbs in a wire basket, plant the sides with small-leaved variegated ivy, and peg the trailing shoots in around the sides to cover the frame with leaves. Then plant medium-height strong-stemmed bulbs like grape hyacinths and *Narcissus* 'Tête-à-Tête' in the centre, with a few dwarf irises (such as *I. reticulata* and *I. danfordiae*) to spread the flowering period. Make sure the basket is hung low enough to be appreciated.

Cascades of gold

Borrow a few plants from the rock garden – always a source of inspiration in spring. Plants with a cascading or trailing habit can sometimes be grown in a basket, though the best results will follow if you leave the baskets planted for a couple of seasons so that the occupants become well established. Gold dust (*Alyssum saxatile*), an easy-to-grow trailer with bright yellow flowers throughout spring, is a good one to start with. Plant several around the sides and one in the top, so that it brims over like a golden cascade.

TUBS AND OTHER CONTAINERS

Tubs, and other containers that hold a generous amount of compost, offer the best scope for a spring display. And because they are less exposed to wind than windowboxes and baskets even the taller bulbs can be grown. Spring-flowering border plants are attractive on their own or as companions for spring bedding plants and bulbs.

Tall tulips

Compact tulips have lots to commend them as container plants, but for sheer elegance it is difficult to beat some of the tall kinds such as Darwin Hybrids and lily-flowered tulips, or the exuberant flamboyance of parrot tulips with their fringed petals and often intriguing petal markings of green or some contrasting colour, such as red on yellow. Most of these taller kinds grow to 45–60 cm (1½–2 ft), but look in proportion in a half-barrel or a deep terracotta pot. They are greatly improved by underplanting with a lower-growing spring bedding plant to clothe the base, which will also extend the flowering period. Dwarf wallflowers are a popular choice, but forget-me-nots are also good. These provide better cover than plants like double daisies and polyanthus.

Colour combinations make all the difference. If planting wallflowers with single colour tulips, pick a single colour wallflower that either harmonizes or contrasts, such as a pale yellow wallflower like 'Primrose Bedder' with dark pink tulips, or deep blue forget-me-nots with yellow tulips. Try white tulips underplanted with blue grape hyacinths.

Tulips with a difference

Low, shallow, dish-like containers and low troughs are best planted with compact tulips. In a windy or exposed site, early doubles are especially useful. Mixtures are best planted with something blue, such as forget-me-nots, to act as a contrast and a unifying theme among a riot of bright and often conflicting colours. If you want to create special colour schemes, separate varieties are available in all the usual tulip colours.

Some of the species tulips and their hybrids can look a little stiff and formal in containers, but *T. praestans* 'Fusilier' is an outstanding bright red, with heads of two to four flowers that give it a far more informal appearance. Try planting white *Anemone blanda* or *A. nemorosa* beneath to emphasize the brilliant scarlet of the tulips.

It is difficult to improve on *T. praestans* 'Fusilier', but *T. p.* 'Unicum' is almost identical in flower and has the bonus of wonderful creamy yellow edges to the leaves: guaranteed to attract comment long before the flowers appear.

There are other variegated tulips. 'Esperanto' is a Viridiflora variety with leaves edged silvery white. Try underplanting it with white arabis or white double daisies (*Bellis perennis*). These will echo the variegation and act as a wonderful foil for the tulips: deep china rose flowers heavily flushed green.

Dazzling daffodils

A tub or half barrel packed with daffodils needs no embellishment. By stacking the bulbs one layer above the other, it is possible to achieve the sort of dense display normally associated with established clumps in the garden. In a large and ornate terracotta container nothing else is needed. In a half-barrel you could plant something bushy around the edge, such as forget-me-nots, but if you use any of the large-flowered daffodils it is often best to let them make their own bold statement.

Daffodils are unattractive once flowering has finished, so lift them and replant in a spare piece of ground to die back naturally. Put something else in the container immediately – a group of small evergreen shrubs if it is too soon for summer bedding.

A barrel of fragrance

Plant to please the nose as well as the eye. Some spring-flowering bulbs, such as *Iris danfordiae,* and a few spring perennials that you might use, like primroses, have some fragrance, but it is subtle and the flower has to be sniffed to be appreciated. The wallflower has no modesty and comes to greet you with its powerful scent. Every garden deserves a trough or a tub of wallflowers on the patio or by the door. Use dwarf varieties to underplant around tall bulbs, but grow at least one container of concentrated scent by cramming it with nothing but wallflowers – dwarf varieties if the trough is small, but tall ones if it is a large container like a half-barrel. Provided the plants have been well grown and were pinched out to make them bushy, the impact will be long-lasting and fragrant as well as colourful. Many people prefer to grow mixed colours, but a single-colour, perhaps deep red or bright yellow, can have even more impact.

Use dwarf bulbs to add an extra dash of colour around the base of spring-flowering shrubs such as camellias. Here dwarf daffodils 'February Gold' and Crocus chrysanthus *add to the charm of* Camellia × williamsii *'Golden Spangles'.*

Polyanthus are ideal spring bedding plants for a shallow dish-like container. Mixtures are bright and cheerful (this one is 'Spring Song') and the flowers will last for weeks.

BRING IN THE RESERVES

Bulbs are bright and beautiful but they are also brief in their display. Even the relatively long-flowering types such as grape hyacinths are over in a matter of weeks, while many summer container plants bloom for months. The overall period over which the different species and varieties will flower is respectable, however, and only a little deceit is required to keep your boxes and troughs blooming for a month or more.

Pot up plenty of bulbs, both different varieties of the same kind, such as hyacinths or tulips, making sure you include early, mid-season and late varieties, or a selection of different kinds that flower early (such as snowdrops). Keep the pots in a cold frame or in a sheltered position in the garden, preferably plunged into the soil so that they are less likely to dry out. Use these to replace bulbs in your containers that have finished flowering, or to fill in vacant spaces among permanent plantings.

It is tempting to plant up complete windowboxes or spare tubs or troughs to rotate with those on show, but planting individual pots is much more successful, as you can choose those plants coming into flower at the same time.

Often the whole pot can be plunged into the container to fill a gap, but if the pot is too large or too deep simply knock the plants out of the pot and squeeze the root-ball into the vacant space. If necessary remove a little compost from the bottom or from around the sides.

JOBS FOR SPRING

Summer is when containers are most glorious, with brilliant colours and exotic or stunning flowers. But all this is only possible if the right actions are taken in spring. Even before planting or sowing, there is the essential, but pleasurable, job of planning and ordering.

- **Buy seeds** if not already done. Most bedding plants can still be sown in early or mid spring. Those sown late will be less advanced than those sown in late winter or bought as plants in garden centres, but they usually continue later into the season – an equally valuable attribute.

  Buying plants in late spring or early summer saves time and effort, but for special varieties or the more unusual plants you need to order direct from a seed company so that you can sow your own. Make a point of ordering seeds of a few promising plants that you have not tried before.

- **Order bulbs and tender perennials.** Garden centres offer plenty of basic bulbs like lilies and begonias, but you may have to send to bulb merchants for the less common kinds like nerines (plant now for autumn interest).

  Some bulb merchants also sell the more exotic patio or conservatory plants, like abutilons, daturas, and *Lantana camara* grafted as standards, as well as interesting and uncommon half-hardy trailers such as *Scaevola aemula*, even though these are not bulbous plants. Alternatively you may have to send away to a nursery that specializes in conservatory and tender plants.

- **Plan your summer containers on paper** so that you know what to order. Containers planted on impulse are seldom as satisfactory as those planned and planted with thought. Use some of the summer suggestions in this book as a starting point, and develop these to suit your own tastes.

  In mild areas, summer containers can be planted and put out in late spring. In cold areas wait until early summer. If in doubt, be guided by when the local parks department put out their summer bedding.

- **Plant up summer baskets**, to allow the plants to become established before you put the basket out. Keep baskets in the greenhouse or conservatory for a couple of weeks, then if possible harden the plants off gradually by standing the baskets in a sheltered position outside before hanging them up.

CHAPTER 2

SUMMER SPECTACLES

SUMMER BRINGS a cornucopia of colour, with flowers tumbling from baskets and windowboxes, and shrubs like fuchsias and clematis flowering enthusiastically in tubs and troughs. The problem is not finding suitable plants but deciding which you have space to grow.

Some enthusiasts prefer to try all new plants each year in an urgent quest for the exotic or the uncommon; others prefer to stick to the tried and tested like pelargoniums (geraniums) and combinations such as alyssum and lobelia. The first group is likely to have many failures and every season will be an unknown, the second group will always have a dependable show but it will lack imagination. A more sensible compromise is to grow plenty of old favourites for the backbone of your display, along with less common plants that you have tried and liked, but to try something a little different too.

Experiment with annuals but plant a tree or a large and striking foliage plant such as *Phormium tenax* or a truly stunning datura, with giant, scented flowers that hang like bells on big, bushy plants. You do not have to spend a lot of money for a striking and tropical-looking foliage plant for your patio – for the cost of a packet of seeds you can grow the castor oil plant (*Ricinus communis*) which combines big leaf size with attractive red, bronze and purple colouring . . . and possibly a few unusual bright red flowers. Several tender perennials, such as the fluorescent daisy wheels of the South African gerberas and the scarlet trumpets of the Chilean glory vine, can be raised from seed to lend an exotic glory for a season.

WINDOWBOXES

Windowboxes should be brim full of colour for as long as possible. It is difficult to create the right impression with windowboxes beneath every window during the winter, but make a stunning impression by fixing matching windowboxes for every window during the summer. Make sure all the boxes have the same style and match the architecture of the house.

Attempts at an integrated look will fail dismally if all the windowboxes are planted differently, so choose the same plants for each windowbox – use mixed colours of the same plant for variety, or mix different kinds but keep to the same planting plan for each box.

DON'T FORGET FOLIAGE

Foliage effect is particularly important. Plants with large, bold leaves like phormiums and acanthus make a special kind of dramatic statement, but foliage is also important in summer windowboxes and other containers. Use silver and gold foliage among the flowers; grow a few silver-foliaged shrubs in containers so that you can move them around to wherever a contrast with bright flowers or vivid foliage is required.

Single-subject stunners

Try keeping the planting simple by using just one kind of plant. This can be more striking than a complex mixture of different annuals, as anyone who has seen the way the Swiss, Germans and French use cascade geraniums (pelargoniums) so effectively will know. The effect is almost breathtakingly beautiful.

Choose plants with a cascading or bushy habit and some height if planting only one kind. Very neat, compact plants like fibrous-rooted begonias (*Begonia semperflorens*) will not provide enough cover in relation to box. These can work in a very shallow box for a small window (try alternate plants of a white-flowered variety with bronze foliage and a red-flowered one with green foliage). For a windowbox of more generous proportions use a bushier type of begonia such as the Non-stop range.

Petunias are usually sold as mixtures but seed is available for separate colours too, and you can choose one to blend with the container or to contrast with it.

Few plants can sustain the flowering power of impatiens (busy Lizzies) and pelargoniums (geraniums), however, and both will bloom from early summer until brought to an abrupt end by frost. For a balcony or upstairs windowbox, grow one of the petunias with a cascading habit (such as 'Super Cascade') or varieties of ivy-leaved or cascade geraniums, which can be enjoyed from below as well as above.

Try a late sowing of a bright red salvia. Grow the plants on in spare plastic windowboxes in an unused but light part of the garden, but be sure to pinch out the growing tips while the plants are still small, to make them bushy. Having been started late, they will look their best in late summer and will continue to provide an eye-catching splash of brilliant red right into autumn, after the main flush of the summer bedding plants have either died or are looking decidedly jaded.

Opposite: *If the container is elegant, restrained planting can be more effective than a mass of bloom. This cordyline is just softened around the base with an ivy.*

Medleys of colour

Single-subject planting can look tasteful and even bold, but a well-planted mixed windowbox, bursting with flowers and long cascading trailers will be more of a crowd-puller. The most effective nearly always contain a mixture of the most traditional bedding plants: petunias, geraniums, pansies and trailing lobelia. A couple of French marigolds will bring a few splashes of bold yellow.

Tuberous-rooted begonias are useful for a mixed arrangement. Three begonias in mixed colours, perhaps yellow, white and red, a couple of blue cascading petunias, and one or two plants of an orange busy Lizzie with bronze foliage will fill quite a large box with colour. To fill in any gaps or to create a more cascading effect, add two or three silver-leaved *Helichrysum petiolare*.

Be restrained. Do not try to cram in too many different kinds of plants. A mixture of three or four kinds will be more effective than half a dozen, which can just look a jumble. If you want to add more, use a foliage plant for contrast, such as the grey-leaved *Cineraria maritima* or *Pyrethrum ptarmicaeflorum* (both with silver leaves) or *P.* 'Golden Ball' (a ball of yellow foliage).

PICK YOUR PARTNERS

Be careful about the partners you marry together. Most nasturtiums will swamp their partners, and after a short time they will be the dominant partner, and may even smother the other plants. If you want to use nasturtiums choose trailing varieties or very compact ones, and in either case keep the shoots pinched back as necessary.

Variation in height is useful, but avoid planting a tall and vigorous plant next to a compact one that will be overshadowed. Instead of planting a tall African marigold next to a compact fibrous-rooted begonia, choose a compact French marigold; for a blue, an ageratum would be a more appropriate companion than a spreading petunia. Use trailers such as ivies or *Helichrysum petiolare* to extend the eye downwards, and a few silver-leaved foliage plants like *Pyrethrum ptarmicaeflorum* to add a little unobtrusive height among the flowers.

Pinks and reds

For a fiery effect, try a combination of a spiky brilliant scarlet *Salvia splendens* ('Red Riches' and 'Carabiniere' are good ones) with sugar pink verbena 'Pink Panther' to provide the feathery infill. In a large box, use a few grey-leaved plants such as *Cineraria maritima* to provide relief and contrast.

The Non-stop range of tuberous begonias can sometimes be bought as separate colours. Interplant red and pink ones, or use a mass of red *or* pink tuberous begonias for the main display with the fibrous-rooted 'Pink Avalanche' to fill out the front.

Fibrous-rooted begonias are also useful for bold, even jarring combinations. Choose separate colours from the Olympia or Danica ranges. The pinks and reds together may not appeal to everyone, but are worth experimenting with: try combining 'Olympia Pink' with 'Pink Avalanche'.

Hot oranges and flame

For a really fiery display keep to one kind of plant. Grow a boxful of nasturtium 'Whirlybird Scarlet', or 'Alaska Mixed' (this has a good range of reds and oranges, with the merit of white-splashed leaves to cool them off).

There are orange-red petunias that are truly eye-catching, like 'Supermagic Orange'.

Blues and mauves

Blue makes a cool, refreshing change from all the hot colours, and a windowbox that has all blue and mauve shades can be particularly appealing as a contrast among the brighter colours. If there is enough room in the box to introduce some foliage plants too, use silver-greys like the trailing *Helichrysum petiolare* and *Pyrethrum ptarmicaeflorum*.

Petunias are always worth including because they flower well for a long time. Separate blue varieties are available, such as 'Blue Joy' (a multiflora), 'Supermagic Light Blue' and 'Supermagic Mid Blue' (grandifloras). Mix them with blue ageratums, blue lobelias and blue pansies. If you are not using silver-leaved foliage plants to break up the colours, choose appropriate variations in shades of blue.

TRUE BLUE?

Beware of colour illustrations in books and catalogues when choosing which blue varieties to buy. Blue is a notoriously difficult colour to photograph, as film registers this colour in a different way from the eye, and unless special filters are used blues often look too pink or magenta. Photographs of ageratum and lobelia are often wildly inaccurate, so whenever possible make your notes for future years from personal observation.

Yellows and whites

French marigolds come in all shades of yellow, but unless you grow one of the Afro-French or triploid varieties (such as 'Zenith Sunset' or 'Nell Gwyn') which are larger and bushier, mix them with other plants to provide more contrast of shape and height. Yellow or white pansies combine well, and *Calceolaria rugosa* 'Sunshine' will help to fill in the background. The small chrysanthemum *Matricaria eximia* 'Butterball' is also worth incorporating, with its small yellow pom-pom flowers on compact plants all summer long. If you want to introduce a touch of white, add a few plants of *M. e.* 'Snow Dwarf'.

For a touch of country garden elegance as a change from the more garish bedding plants, try the white daisy-like marguerite (*Chrysanthemum frutescens*) mixed with a yellow variety like 'Jamaica Primrose' in a large windowbox. They will flower for months and have a delicate charm for a country cottage window-sill or trough that needs no enhancement from other plants.

Ordinary bedding dahlias are totally unsuitable for windowboxes, but the Lilliput range makes a refreshing change from the more common windowbox plants, and alternate plants of 'Bambino' (creamy yellow) and 'Little John' (bright yellow) create a really mellow effect.

Tumbling down

Do not mask an attractive hand-painted or decorated windowbox, or one with pretty tiles or panels, with masses of trailing plants. Let the box itself add to the decorative effect.

Inexpensive windowboxes, and unattractive wooden ones, however, are best covered with cascading plants. Trailing pelargoniums (geraniums), cascading begonias, variegated ground ivy (*Glechoma hederacea* 'Variegata'), *Helichrysum petiolare*, trailing verbenas, and cascading fuchsias and lobelias are the most useful.

Adding a little height

Windows that open outwards limit the height of plants that you can include, and the boxes often have to be placed on brackets beneath the windows. Sash-type windows that slide up and down offer more scope for the use of vertical space. Taller 'dot' plants, such as the burning bush (*Kochia trichophylla*) and heliotropes (*Heliotropium peruvianum*) can be used to punctuate the arrangement and bring a little extra height. With the use of a small plastic trellis set behind the windowbox, small climbers can be used, which will look good from inside or out if you do not mind sacrificing a little light. Enjoy the sight and smell of sweet peas by growing one of the dwarf kinds that grow to about 90 cm (3 ft). 'Jet Set' and 'Knee-Hi' are popular varieties; 'Continental Mixed' is one of the best.

Something different

Almost any plant of a suitable size can be grown in a windowbox, but experiment with a healthy scepticism. There is so much choice in the summer that you should only give space to plants that will provide lots of colour over a long period.

An all-fuchsia windowbox can be created with upright compact varieties like 'Tom Thumb' for the back of the box, and cascading varieties tumbling over the front, but why not be even more individual with a box of the fuchsia-like *Phygelius aquaelis*? The orange-buff tubular flowers are produced from mid summer through to mid autumn. 'Yellow Trumpets' is a particularly charming variety with yellow flowers.

A box planted with *Lantana camara* is always eye-catching, with its ball-like clusters of red, yellow, orange, pink and white flowers. A box of these mixed colours can hardly fail to impress.

A windowbox of trailing carnations sounds unlikely, but dwarf and slightly cascading forms of these fragrant plants can be obtained. Keep deadheading them to prolong flowering.

For an all-blue effect, plant up the box with the blue daisy-like *Felicia amelloides*, and plant the magnificent blue trailer *Scaevola aemula* to tumble down the front.

BASKETS

Select a sunny, sheltered position for your baskets. A shady, windswept site will almost certainly bring disappointment.

Some of the finest baskets can be seen in towns where a parks department has acquired the special skills and resources required. The baskets may be twice the size of those sold to amateurs (after all they can hang theirs on strong lamp-posts!), and often contain water reservoirs. There may be as many as a dozen different kinds of plants in some of these baskets, but you cannot hope to imitate this kind of planting in a small basket, and half a dozen different kinds is about the limit for a 30 cm (12 in) basket. On a small scale a single-subject basket is often just as effective as one planted with as many different plants as it is possible to cram in.

Tubs have a dwarfing effect on shrubs, and even plants that grow large in a border, like this rhododendron 'Pink Pearl', will remain compact for many years.

Balls of beauty

Use a wire basket with a liner that is easy to plant through (such as moss or black polythene) to create a ball of bloom. Plastic baskets with solid sides, and hanging pots, are unsuitable. The plants suggested here are not true trailers (these would produce a curtain-like effect rather than a ball), so you need to plant in the sides as well as the top.

Widely available plants to use include fibrous-rooted begonias (*Begonia semperflorens*), busy Lizzies (impatiens), pansies and lobelia. Mixed colours of lobelia are especially effective; use a compact variety such as 'Kaleidoscope' or 'Mixed Shades' for a tight ball, or a trailing variety, such as 'Cascade Mixed' or 'Fountain Mixture' for a looser effect.

Less common annuals that also make a pretty ball of colour are Swan River daisies (*Brachycome iberidifolia*), *Calceolaria* 'Midas', *Nolana* 'Shooting Star', creeping zinnia (*Sanvitalia procumbens*), and *Coleus* 'Scarlet Poncho'. The coleus is a foliage plant, but its large scarlet leaves edged green and gold match flowers for colour and impact. Most coleus are unsuitable for baskets, but this one has a useful cascading habit. Outdoors, it needs a bright but sheltered position.

Cascades of colour

Long trailing strands of foliage and tumbling flowers epitomize a hanging basket for many, but this effect is quite difficult to achieve outdoors. Those plants that are tough and fast-growing, like trailing nasturtiums, are likely to swamp other plants, while many foliage plants that cascade without threatening their companions often produce a muted effect rather than a curtain of colour. Those that usually perform well include variegated ground ivy (*Glechoma hederacea* 'Variegata') and yellow-flowered creeping Jenny (*Lysimachia nummularia*) and its gold-leaved variety 'Aurea'.

If you have a conservatory in which you can keep the basket protected from frost during the winter, Swedish ivies are excellent for foliage effect. There are several green and variegated forms, but *Plectranthus coleoides* 'Marginatus' and *P. oertendahlii* are two of the best, both with white variegation and trailing shoots that will soon hang for a metre (yard) or more in protected conditions. If hardened off properly they can be used in outdoor baskets.

Ordinary variegated ivies are useful for softening the outline of a hanging basket, but do not expect sheets of trailing foliage within the few months that a summer basket is in position.

Showering flowers

A showering effect, with sprays of flowers tumbling over the edge of the basket is much easier to achieve than long curtains of foliage or flowers, and more practical where long trailers are likely to get in the way, such as near a front door. Some plants, such as cascading fuchsias, may in any case tumble far below the base of the basket.

Fuchsias and geraniums (pelargoniums) must be high on any list of good basket plants, either on their own or mixed with other plants. Fuchsias are best in single-subject baskets: some of their beauty and elegance is lost amid a mass of other foliage and flowers. For a showering basket you will need three or five plants, depending on basket size, spaced around the edge. Choose a cascading variety such as 'Cascade' and angle the rootball when you plant to encourage the cascading effect from an early stage. If you have a large basket, use an upright fuchsia in the middle with cascading varieties around the edge.

Ivy-leaved geraniums are useful in a mixed basket, but use the Continental Cascade type for a really stunning geraniums-only basket. These produce tumbling shoots about 45 cm (18 in) long.

Hanging (Pendula) begonias flower for months, and are available in a wide range of colours as tubers. Pack plenty in the basket for a really bold show.

Trailing lobelia and verbena can also make a basket look as though it is dripping colour.

Mixing and matching

Mixed baskets create a different impression entirely. The basket appears to burst with colour in all directions, and the overall effect is more important than individual plants. The less dominant plants are sometimes almost hidden, but they still contribute to the overall impression. Even one or two individual flowers poking through the dominant kinds serve as punctuation points.

The combinations are unlimited and exact planting plans must reflect the size of your baskets and the plants available. The suggestions below can be used without modification or adapted to suit the plants available and your own taste.

Balls of light and shade Yellow, white and blue petunias (three separate colours), with yellow, white and blue pansies. Plant the sides as well as the top.

Reds and yellows Red upright geraniums and yellow tagetes with *Calceolaria rugosa* 'Midas' (also yellow) in the top, and trailing red and yellow nasturtiums below.

Cascading fuchsias and lobelia Plant bright red cascading fuchsias with deep blue compact or trailing lobelia.

Silvers and pinks Pink double geraniums and grey-leaved *Helichrysum petiolare*.

Spots of orange Pink and purple petunias with red and blue lobelia, relieved by the bright orange flowers of black-eyed Susan (*Thunbergia alata*).

Multicoloured magic If the basket is large, break the rules and try packing in lots of different plants rather than several plants of a few kinds. Pack in as many as you can from the following: white petunias, pink ivy-leaved geraniums, red 'Breakaway' geraniums, blue trailing lobelia, yellow *Calceolaria rugosa* 'Midas', grey-leaved *Cineraria maritima*, and the silver foliaged *Helichrysum microphyllum*.

Red, white and blue White alyssum, blue lobelia, red busy Lizzies (impatiens). Only suitable for a basket where planting in the sides is practical, otherwise the mixed red, white and blue effect is difficult to achieve.

Another compact red, white and blue arrangement would be white and red varieties of fibrous-rooted begonias with blue compact lobelia or ageratum. For a more informal, cascading effect, use trailing blue lobelia, cascading red fuchsias (or red petunias), and white petunias.

HALF-BASKETS AND WALL POTS

Half-baskets, sometimes called wall baskets, hold less compost than equivalent hanging baskets but the display is often just as brilliant. Hanging baskets are better if they have an open position, or are on a long bracket that enables them to be turned every day or two. If this is not possible they become one-sided anyway with only one decent 'face', and a wall basket or pot would look just as good.

For a foaming mass of flowers with colour tumbling over the edge and down the wall, a wire or plastic half-basket is adequate, as you see only the flowers once the plants are established. The drawbacks come at the end of summer. Winter and spring arrangements will not mask the container so well, especially if it has been replanted in the autumn. If you choose this kind of container you either put up with rather inelegant containers while spring-flowering bulbs are growing, or take them down and give winter a miss.

Terracotta wall pots are generally more attractive, and some are ornate enough to look good even when the planting is sparse. But make sure you choose a design that holds enough compost. If a terracotta wall pot is attractively decorated, plant with restraint. Pansies and violas, busy Lizzies (impatiens), and fibrous-rooted begonias are all suitable. If you need something with a looser habit that will tumble a little without obliterating the decoration, many verbenas, such as 'Sissinghurst' and 'Cleopatra', will fit the bill. 'Peaches and Cream' is a more upright verbena but nevertheless loose enough in outline to fill the container without looking too 'clumpy'. The flowers open deep coral and age through shades of creamy-yellow to salmon and apricot. This delicate colour combination on the one plant makes it a beautiful choice for a terracotta wall pot, perhaps with blue ageratum or blue lobelia as a contrast.

HANGING POTS

Some hanging pots are made of terracotta and can be quite pleasing, but most are plastic with hangers of the same material. These are functional but hardly aesthetically pleasing. They are widely used for many kinds of plants, including the piggy-back plant (*Tolmeia menziesii*) and busy Lizzies. They are useful for displaying this kind of plant in a conservatory, where the plants have to be in some sort of container anyway, but outdoors these plants are better in the ground or a more attractive pot.

Opposite: *Do not be afraid to use a few less conventional basket plants along with the more traditional summer bedding. In addition to alyssum, impatiens, lobelia, pansies and variegated ground ivy (Glechoma hederacea 'Variegata'), this one contains a tradescantia and variegated tolmiea, more usually seen as houseplants.*

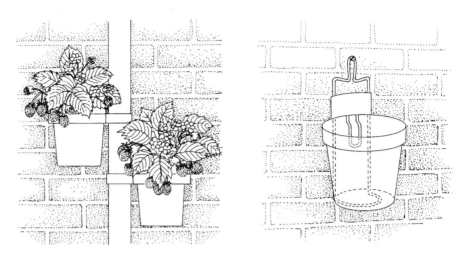

Fig 1 *Make the most of available space with supports like these, which will hold a 15–18 cm (6–7 in) plant pot. The one on the left is designed to fit around a standard 64 mm (2½ in) plastic drainpipe; the one on the right can be screwed to a solid wall or a wooden fence.*

Hanging pots are useful for single specimens of cascading plants, such as trailing campanulas, some of the cascading tradescantias that can be used outdoors in the summer, and annuals such as nasturtiums.

As well as purpose-made hanging pots, ordinary pots can be slid into wall hangers that are screwed into the house wall, or fixed to a drainpipe (Fig. 1), and the same general advice about suitable plants applies to these.

TUBS AND OTHER CONTAINERS

Tubs and troughs are often larger and heavier than baskets and windowboxes, and they can be used in a position that suits the plant. You can give them full sun or shade all day if that is what the plants require. Because weight is not a problem (except for balcony and roof gardens), loam-based compost can be used and this means that shrubs and small trees can be grown, too.

Except for autumn and winter containers, for which compromise is inevitable, choose perennials that can remain in the container for at least two or three years, and possibly longer, with suitable feeding and topdressing (see pages 107–8).

The plant combinations suggested for windowboxes and hanging baskets can be used for tubs and troughs with the exception of very long trailers such as trailing nasturtiums (use a bush variety instead). In addition, some of the taller bedding plants, like African marigolds, night-flowering nicotianas and even dwarf sweet peas can be used, along with the larger striking annual foliage plants such as the castor oil plant (*Ricinus communis*).

Use tubs and similar large containers for large backbone plants, reserving some of them for permanent plantings (see Chapter 5), to give your container garden a sense of continuity and permanence. It is often possible to plant around the base with seasonal spring and summer bedding.

Hardy shrubs

Trees and shrubs remain compact in containers. A rhododendron that might reach 3 m (10 ft) or more in the garden will take many years to grow more than 1.8 m (6 ft), and trees are likely to achieve only half their normal height and growth rate. This makes it possible to grow many that would otherwise appear far too large for a patio or balcony, but choose carefully and wherever possible grow compact species and varieties. Even though the growth of a tree or shrub will be restricted in a container, do not try to get away with a small pot or tub. Most of the suggestions below require a tub at least 45 cm (18 in) in diameter: a half-barrel is ideal.

Avoid too many foliage evergreens, such as conifers and box, otherwise the garden will be dull and predictable. Introduce a few flowering shrubs: even if they are uninspiring for most of the summer, and their bare branches decidedly boring in the winter, they give a patio or balcony garden the sense of structure and permanence that they do in a shrub border. When they do burst into bloom they make a contribution equal to that of seasonal bedding plants. Flowering shrubs also tend to look better year by year as they mature – and are much less demanding than seasonal plants.

If you have a favourite summer-flowering shrub it may be worth trying it in a large tub, but the following are reliable shrubs to start with.

Buddleia (butterfly bush) Plant this for the beauty of the bush and for the butterflies that it will attract. Prune each spring to keep the plant compact and flowering well.

Plant around the base with an evergreen ground cover, such as ivy or *Pachysandra terminalis* 'Variegata'. Let spring-flowering bulbs such as grape hyacinths grow through the ground cover – these will provide early interest.

Hebe (shrubby veronica) Invaluable evergreen foliage plants, but some are worth growing for their flowers too. 'Midsummer Beauty', 'Marjorie', and 'Autumn Glory' have attractive flowers and bloom for a very long period. The latter, as its name suggests, continues well into autumn.

Unfortunately hebes are not reliably hardy in cold areas. Most will survive normal winters without protection in favourable areas, but an exceptionally cold winter may kill them. Plants in containers are more vulnerable than those in the ground, so move them into a cold greenhouse or a conservatory for the winter, or give them some winter protection outdoors (see page 109).

For a quick burst of colour, plant spring and autumn-flowering crocuses around the base and leave them undisturbed to multiply.

Hydrangea Hydrangeas make good tub plants, despite their need for plenty of water. They look especially good in a half-barrel, with a good reservoir of compost, where they thrive provided watering is not neglected. The acidity of the compost is easily controlled, so it is not difficult to achieve good colouring unaffected by alkaline soil.

A well-grown hydrangea will bush out from the base so underplanting is difficult once the plant is well established, but plant a ground cover of ivy to trail over the side of the tub.

Lavender These are shrubs best seen *en masse* and not as individual plants, but find space for one on the patio, perhaps by a seat, where you can brush against it to release the distinctive lavender aroma. Lavenders come in various shades of blues, purples and even pinks; most have attractive evergreen grey foliage.

Plant a few garden pinks around the lavender (choose a pink variety such as 'Doris'). The colour combination is good, and the two fragrances make this a container for a special spot near a garden seat.

Philadelphus (mock orange) The flowering period is relatively short, but the really strong scent compensates. Take your pick from a selection of readily available varieties, with single or double white flowers, but choose a compact one such as 'Belle Etoile'.

Mock oranges can make quite bushy, spreading shrubs, so underplanting does not work well. Extend the season by planting a late-flowering clematis, such as *C. viticella* 'Abundance', to climb through the philadelphus.

Rhododendron If you like rhododendrons but your garden soil is alkaline, grow them in containers. Even those that grow very large in the garden, such as 'Pink Pearl', make good container plants. The Yakushimanum hybrids, which are naturally compact, are especially good in containers.

Plant in a loam-based ericaceous compost (although they appreciate peat, most peat-based composts will have had lime added to make them less acid).

Most rhododendrons bridge the gap between spring and summer. Concentrate any underplanting to provide autumn interest. Not much will grow around the base of an old specimen, but autumn crocuses (colchicums) will grow well while the rhododendron is still young.

Roses Roses are much happier in beds, but on a balcony, or in a courtyard garden, growing them in containers may be the only option. Choose low-growing varieties of floribundas or hybrid teas – those described in some catalogues as patio roses are likely to be the most appropriate. If you want to underplant, dwarf spring-flowering bulbs, polyanthus and pansies all work well. For summer cover around the base, pansies are bright without detracting too much from the roses. You could choose a contrasting colour, say blue pansies around a yellow rose.

Rambling and climbing roses are good candidates for a container on a balcony or in a backyard where there is no opportunity to plant in the ground. Place the container against the wall and train the plant up a large trellis or other support.

Spiraea There are many species and varieties to grow, including some pretty white-flowered species for the spring, but the one usually planted for summer interest is S. × *bumalda* and its varieties. 'Anthony Waterer' is one of the most popular for flowers, but 'Goldflame' is a better all-round variety because its foliage is attractive all summer. S. × *bumalda* will bush well from the base if pruned appropriately, and is best grown on its own.

Tender but tough

Some of the finest container shrubs are too tender to be left unprotected through the average winter, but if you have somewhere to overwinter them, or in some cases are prepared to protect them outdoors, they are worth the effort.

Fuchsias have all the qualities of a first-rate container plant, and flower from early summer until well into autumn. For troughs, windowboxes and hanging baskets, young plants raised from cuttings are usually used, but as a centrepiece for a large tub more mature plants overwintered in a greenhouse or conservatory are more impressive. Standards in particular have to be treated in this way as they take years to train and are vulnerable in winter. If this is too much trouble, there are a few fairly hardy species, such as *F. magellanica* and its hybrids, that will survive outdoors, though in cold areas they will be cut down to ground level.

Use plenty of trailing plants to hide the front of a windowbox. This one contains nasturtiums and lobelia to break the hard line, sharing the space with geraniums (pelargoniums) and fuchsias . . . with a few dashes of silver foliage provided by Cineraria maritima.

These are less spectacular than the large-flowered hybrids however, and not such useful container plants. The grey-leaved *Helichrysum petiolare* is a good foil for the bright fuchsia flowers, and it will tumble over the edge of the container.

The marguerite, *Chrysanthemum frutescens*, now becoming widely sold under its more recent name of *Argyranthemum frutescens*, is an outstanding evergreen sub-shrub that ought to be in every collection of container plants. In window-boxes and troughs bush forms are best, but for a pot or tub, choose one trained as a standard, which will have a ball of daisy-like blooms on a long stem all summer, below which you can plant all the usual summer-flowering annuals. Bush forms are usually raised from cuttings and are not very expensive to buy afresh each spring, but standards are expensive enough to make it worth over-wintering them in a greenhouse or conservatory. Try a pair of standards in 30 cm (12 in) pots on their own, one either side of the door.

Oleander (*Nerium oleander*) may bring back memories of Mediterranean holidays, with its terminal clusters of pretty pink flowers set against leathery evergreen foliage. It makes a pretty patio plant for a large tub, but requires over-wintering inside so avoid a container that is difficult to lift easily. Too much winter warmth is detrimental and a cool but frost-free greenhouse or conservatory is ideal.

Make the most of walls

For a balcony or a paved garden where it is difficult to plant climbers in the soil, the use of vertical space is especially important. There are plenty of perennials and annual climbers to use, provided you give them a suitable support.

A trellis, or galvanized wires fixed to the wall (Fig. 2a and b), will provide a suitable support for most climbers. Simply place the container against the wall and tie the climber to the support to start it off. Less substantial supports are adequate for most annual climbers. A plastic trellis can be inserted into a large tub (Fig. 2c), even canes will do for sweet peas, and you can make a trough that includes a built-in wooden trellis for small climbers.

Almost all annual climbers can be grown successfully in containers, and some of the best for a patio are canary creeper (*Tropaeolum canariense*) with its fringed yellow flowers, morning glory (*Convolvulus major*, *Ipomoea rubro-caerulea* 'Heavenly Blue'), and sweet peas.

Climbing roses, provided they are not too rampant a type, are often successful in large containers, or for something a little different, grow a collection of large-flowered clematis (not a very vigorous species such as *C. montana*) in a half-barrel, training them up a wigwam of canes (Fig. 2d). Choose three different varieties for a succession of bloom.

On a balcony, or in a paved backyard or tiny town garden, clever use of the walls themselves is important. Paint them a light colour (white or a pastel shade such as pale pink) to reflect light and show off the plants. Take advantage of their shelter and residual warmth to include a few of the more uncommon kinds of climber and wall shrub and the garden will be that much more 'special' and interesting.

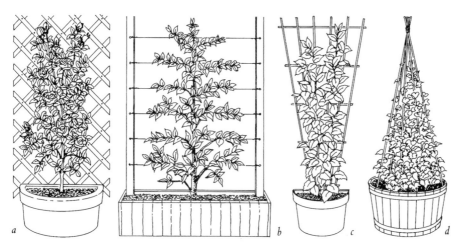

Fig 2 *Tall plants and most climbers require some form of support. The easiest method is to fix a trellis to the wall (a) and grow the plant in a container that will fit close against it. A frame can be built for a wooden trough (b) to make a free-standing unit with parallel galvanized wires. Fan-shaped metal or plastic trellises (c) are suitable for a compact climber such as a large-flowered clematis. Clematis and runner beans in a half-barrel look good grown up a wigwam of canes (d) secured at the top with string or a proprietary cane holder.*

The New Zealand glory pea (*Clianthus puniceus*) is one of those plants distinctive enough to make visitors stop to admire and enquire. If you have a warm, sunny wall against which to plant it in a large container, its dramatic red, almost claw-shaped flowers will give your garden a touch of distinction. It will grow to about 2.1 m (7 ft) trained against a wall, but of course climbers are not easy to take indoors for the winter so you will have to protect the stems with straw or similar material (see page 109) and mulch around the plant to a depth of about 10 cm (4 in). Protect the roots by wrapping the container with insulation. In all but the coldest areas this is usually sufficient to bring it through relatively unscathed.

The Chilean glory flower (*Eccremocarpus scaber*) is another climber that can be trained against a wall to a similar height. Use it to help brighten up a sunny or shady wall on a balcony or in a courtyard. It will probably be cut down by cold in the winter, but in mild areas the roots will survive to produce new shoots the next year. As the plant is easy to raise from seed as an annual, it is not worth special protection in cold areas.

A passion flower tough enough to try outside with some certainty of success is *Passiflora caerulea*. Planted in the ground it will require no special winter treatment in mild areas, but in a container prune it back to about 1.5 m (5 ft) and take it into a cool greenhouse or conservatory, or even an enclosed porch. Put it out again in spring and train the new shoots up a suitable wall support. Given this treatment you can try other more delicate species such as *P. quadrangularis*.

If you have a conservatory where you can overwinter shrubs that need protection from the cold, plants like this Nerium oleander *will give the patio that exotic touch.*

Fremontodendron 'Californian Glory' is a real eye-catcher with its big yellow blooms that simply ask to be admired. It will survive most winters in all but the coldest areas without difficulty, but how well it thrives depends on how protected the area is. In cold districts it will cover a wall to a height of about 2.4 m (8 ft); in areas with very mild winters it can grow much larger. As plants in tubs are more vulnerable than those in the ground, it is worth insulating the container for the winter.

The tropical touch

Create a tropical effect in a small part of the garden, perhaps a sunny corner of the patio. Many of the plants suggested below are tender, some may already be kept as house or greenhouse plants, and these *must* be hardened off thoroughly. Be especially careful to protect them from cold winds and even strong sunlight when they are first placed outside. Many houseplants benefit from a few months outdoors, but do not risk any particularly prized plant as weather and pests are likely to take their toll by the end of the summer.

Some of the plants below are hardy in many less than tropical climates, but bring a 'tropical' look to the patio or balcony.

Palm-like plants always look good on the patio, but they are best used to add height to a group of plants, or as single specimens framed against a suitable background to form a focal point: a fan palm viewed against a painted wall for example. Add a few tender species from indoors for the summer, but let hardier kinds form the framework.

Trachycarpus fortunei (Chusan or fan palm) is one of those plants hardy enough to thrive in milder areas, where it can grow into a tall tree, but it is too tender to survive many degrees of frost unprotected, and will usually have to be taken indoors for the winter. The dwarf fan palm (*Chamaerops humilis*) is also hardy enough to grow outdoors in very mild regions, but if possible bring it indoors for the winter. If that is not possible, apply a very thick mulch over the top of the compost and insulate the container. Top growth may be killed but if the roots survive the crown may shoot again.

Cordyline australis looks more like a spiky-leaved house plant when young, but with age becomes tree-shaped, with yucca-like leaves at the top of a distinct trunk. It is hardy outside in mild areas, and often thrives in coastal gardens. The purple-leaved form *C. a. purpurea* is especially attractive while young. Cordylines in containers are best moved to a cool greenhouse or conservatory for the winter.

Add a yucca or two, which will enhance the grouping with its stunningly imposing white flower spikes when old enough, and include some bold foliage plants like *Fatsia japonica*, *Rheum palmatum* or even ordinary culinary rhubarb.

Against this background of contrasting foliage shape, add some colour to the picture, first with colourful foliage plants such as *Aeonium arboreum* 'Atropurpureum', *Agave americana* 'Variegata', coleus and even crotons, then spice it all up with bright and flamboyant flowers such as gerberas and cannas.

Make sure the plants are grouped closely together in one corner, then put a stamp of distinction on the effect by adding a datura. These are guaranteed to bring a touch of the tropical to your patio. The bell-like flowers are often 20 cm (8 in) long and almost as broad. Colours are usually white or pink on a bushy plant that easily grows to 1.8 m (6 ft) in a season. These plants are sometimes available in garden centres but can also be ordered by post. They will be killed by frost, however, so they must be overwintered indoors or in a greenhouse . . . and they are large plants to accommodate, even if pruned back first. But the exotic fragrance of their blooms will make any effort seem worthwhile.

Lilies and other bulbs

Lilies have become popular as pot-plants, but those sold in flower by florists and garden centres have probably been specially treated to keep them dwarf. The same varieties grown from bulbs planted in containers in the garden may be a little taller but the effect is just as beautiful. And those bought in flower can be used to provide pockets of instant colour if you failed to plant dormant bulbs. Lilies are among the most exotic-looking summer-flowering bulbs, but they require careful placing. The heads are always bold and beautiful, but the lower parts of the plants are lanky and uninteresting. If using lilies on their own, place the pots behind other containers such as fuchsias and summer bedding to mask the stems (and possibly their supports), or plant the bulbs in the centre of a large tub or half-barrel filled with summer-flowering bedding or herbaceous plants.

The so-called African lily is not a true lily but an agapanthus. These first-rate container plants get better every year as the clump becomes larger and more established. In mild areas you can leave them outdoors (preferably with a little protection when grown in containers), but in most parts they are best moved into a conservatory or greenhouse, or even an enclosed porch. The large, almost globular heads of blue (sometimes white) individual flowers top an attractive clump of strap-shaped foliage. Once a clump is well established it is best on its own in an ornate pot or tub, but while still young try planting white petunias around the base.

Alliums, or ornamental onions, are useful container plants, and there are many summer-flowering kinds that can be grown easily in containers. Some of the most striking of the widely available species are *A. albopilosum* (syn. *A. christophii*) and *A. sphaerocephalum*. Plant close together to create a dense clump for real impact.

Shady subjects

Really shady positions need a careful selection of plants. Even those flowers that tolerate shade, such as busy Lizzies (impatiens), will be taller and more leafy, with fewer flowers than if grown in good light. Place the emphasis on foliage effect, and use some bright short-term pot plants such as vivid gerberas or lilies to provide colour on a rotating basis.

The best bedding plants for shade are busy Lizzies, pansies and fibrous-rooted begonias, which will at least put on a respectable show in a shady spot.

Hostas are good shade plants, but choose those with brightly variegated foliage (the colour may fade as the season progresses). A small collection of say half a dozen different varieties will bring plenty of interest to a dull spot, and many have worthwhile if not spectacular flowers.

Good shrubs for a shady spot are spotted laurel (*Aucuba japonica* varieties), camellias, and the false castor oil plant (*Fatsia japonica*). If you want a ground cover around the base of the shrubs use *Pachysandra terminalis* 'Variegata', which will clothe the compost with its variegated foliage. Try planting spring-flowering bulbs like daffodils and tulips around the base too, although in poor light these will probably require replacing each year.

Herbaceous plants

Herbaceous plants are not ideal for containers, but they add variety and bring their own special charm. Most die down for winter and it is difficult to replant the container because the roots should remain undisturbed. Planting spring bulbs around the edge seldom works well because the space in the middle is taken up by roots from the herbaceous occupant. It is best to choose just a few choice plants and grow them in containers light enough to be moved to an inconspicuous spot during the 'off' season.

Flowering plants that look really good include bear's breeches (*Acanthus mollis* and *A. spinosus*), lady's mantle (*Alchemilla mollis*), astilbes, and some of the euphorbias.

Herbaceous foliage plants to try include hostas in all their various forms, and *Houttuynia cordata* 'Chameleon' – one of the most colourful and outstanding of all foliage plants. Some grasses look good in containers too, but one of the most striking is *Hakonechloa macra* 'Albo-aurea'. Bugle (*Ajuga reptans*) is useful as a carpeter around trees and shrubs in containers, or even at the front of a window-box.

A few herbaceous plants can be mixed with bedding plants very effectively. *Lobelia cardinalis* and the similar *L. fulgens*, with their purple-red foliage and tall spikes of bright red flowers are useful accent plants to introduce height into a tub or trough of summer bedding. *Diascia cordata* is a prostrate perennial with pretty pink flowers, great in a hanging basket, cascading over the edge of a tub, or in a windowbox along with the annuals.

Cheap and cheerful hardy annuals

Hardy annuals that flower where they are sown provide cheap colour. For the cost of a packet of seeds you can fill several windowboxes and troughs with colour. For real cost saving ordinary garden soil can be used instead of compost. Most container plants require the best compost you can provide, but many hardy annuals flower better in poor soil, and as their flowering season is usually relatively brief in comparison to most half-hardy bedding plants it is not necessary to sustain them over a long period.

There are drawbacks. The seeds are not usually sown until late spring, so they start to flower later than most summer bedding plants, and it is difficult to mix them with other kinds of plants which means you are largely confined to single-subject containers. The flowering season is short in comparison with plants like busy Lizzies, geraniums, and fibrous-rooted begonias.

Quick and dependable hardy annuals to sow directly into the container include: anchusa ('Dawn' is a good mixture), calendulas (pot marigolds), candytuft, *Convolvulus minor*, love-in-a-mist (*Nigella*), love-lies-bleeding (*Amaranthus cordatus*), nasturtiums and Virginian stocks.

CO-ORDINATED CONTAINERS

For a 'designer look', plant matching baskets and windowboxes or troughs. On the patio or balcony, a mishmash of plantings and colours can create a jungle-effect and a sense of fun, but for windowboxes and baskets at the front of the house a more restrained approach is usually more appropriate. Try using the same planting combination in a pair of hanging baskets either side of the door and reflect these in the windowboxes. If possible use the same plants again in a trough or tub by the porch. If you can paint the windowboxes to match the colour of the rest of the paint-work, it will look even more coordinated.

JOBS FOR SUMMER

Amid the flush of summer growth and cornucopia of colour the bleaker days of autumn and challenges of winter are easy to dismiss to the back burner of consciousness. Some autumn, winter and spring displays cannot be prepared until the end of summer (especially where they replace summer bedding in the same container), but Planning, Planting and Propagation are the key to successful year-round container gardening . . . and the 'three P's' are as necessary now as at any other season.

- **Sow some annuals for late colour.** Sowing late can help bridge the gap between summer and autumn. Quick-growing annuals such as alyssum, French marigolds, godetia and pansies can be sown in early or mid summer to replenish containers that need a bit of extra interest late in the season as the more advanced plants are flagging. Sow them in pots to fill in gaps, or grow them in spare windowboxes to rotate later.

- **Sow biennials for next year.** For an early display next year sow plenty of biennials in early summer, and grow the seedlings on in a nursery bed (a spare piece of ground) until the autumn. Those invaluable for spring containers include double daisies (*Bellis perennis*), pansies, polyanthus and wallflowers (choose compact varieties). Try to find space for some Brompton stocks, a biennial that helps to bridge the gap between spring and summer flowers.

- **Take cuttings of tender perennials in late summer,** to overwinter as small rooted plants. Geraniums (pelargoniums) and marguerites (*Chrysanthemum frutescens*) are always worth propagating (Fig. 3).

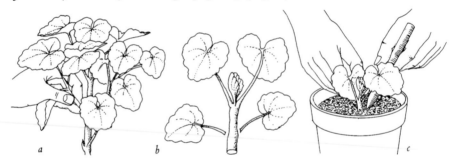

Fig 3 *Geranium (pelargonium) cuttings are easy to root. Choose strong, healthy shoots (**a**), preferably without flowers (though these can be removed). Remove the lower pair of leaves (**b**) with a sharp knife or a razor blade, and pull off the small bract-like stipules at the base of the leaf stalks. Dip the cut ends in a rooting hormone then insert around the edge of a 15 cm (6 in) pot to root (**c**).*

- **Plant permanent arrangements** of shrubs and conifers during the summer, so that they are well established before winter.

- **Buy and plant autumn-flowering bulbs** such as colchicums and true crocuses such as *C. speciosus* and *C. laevigatus* for late colour.

Opposite: *Pale colours make a refreshing change in a garden full of bright colours.* Chrysanthemum (Argyranthemum) frutescens, *with its white daisy-like flowers, makes a happy marriage with* Helichrysum petiolare.

CHAPTER 3

AUTUMN FLING

AUTUMN SHOULD NEVER lack interest or colour, yet containers usually look dejected and neglected at this time. There is a natural inclination to cling on to summer bedding plants until the plants flower themselves to death or the first frost of autumn puts an abrupt and ignominious end to their colourful lives. If containers are replanted, it is usually with spring-flowering bulbs and little else . . . a recipe for some pretty boring containers for the next five or six months.

Some of the suggestions in this chapter may appear expensive because they use berried and foliage shrubs for a display that may last just a couple of months if the containers are to be used for spring and summer displays too. Despite first impressions they are a good investment because such shrubs can be planted in the garden afterwards or used in permanently planted containers. They should give years of pleasure. Sometimes plants from the garden can be lifted for the occasion, but this is seldom as satisfactory as new container-grown plants from a garden centre because the roots have to be hacked about to get the plant to fit the container, and constant lifting and replanting will take its toll. A better way to cut costs is to take cuttings so that you always have a supply of young plants coming along to use in containers.

Autumn-flowering bulbs are invaluable. Plant them in the garden afterwards, where they should grow and multiply, but avoid lifting bulbs from the garden to use in containers unless you know they are large enough to flower – many bulbs and corms flower less dependably the second year because they split into several smaller ones. Once these reach flowering size the display is even better, but in a container display every bulb must flower, as gaps or plants with only leaves are so much more conspicuous in a tub than in a clump in the border. Instead of planting the bulbs in beds and borders afterwards, you can use them in permanently planted containers along with other types of plant, where the odd non-flowering bulb is acceptable.

Nerines are an exception to the rule of planting them out in the garden afterwards. These are best left undisturbed and should be grown as part of a permanent planting or grown in a container of their own and brought into a prominent position for the autumn months (see page 50).

To brighten up those dreary days of late autumn even more, be a little extravagant and buy a few short-term pot-plants such as Cape heathers (*Erica gracilis* and *E. hyemalis*) and year-round pot chrysanthemums even if you have to discard them afterwards. Keep the cost down by using these in just one or two containers in a prominent place, such as by the front door. Concentrate the colour in areas that continue to be used regularly.

Bridging the seasons

There are huge variations in the weather at this time of year, both regionally and from year to year. Favourable areas may not receive their first frost until a couple of months later than the earliest frosts in cold regions. In some years frosts are widespread in mild areas as early as mid autumn, yet in other years it may be early winter before frost cuts its way through the lingering remnants of summer. The differences in both day length and temperature between early and late autumn are considerable: some of the suggested plantings may be appropriate for early autumn but not late autumn, and vice versa.

Plants that perform well in late autumn will probably continue to be attractive into early winter, and these are especially useful. Although this book is divided into seasons for ease of use, there is inevitably a welcome overlap.

HANGING BASKETS

Specially planted autumn baskets are seldom very successful, and replanting in autumn is even more difficult: by the time the plants are established the weather is usually becoming too severe and the plants do not look happy. Baskets are

BE BOLD WITH A FUN BASKET

Most keen gardeners would find the idea of artificial flowers an anathema, though it has to be said that most of these are so realistic nowadays that even gardening enthusiasts can be fooled at times. What looks really bad, however, is artificial flowers and foliage at the wrong season (summer flowers in winter, for example). A 'contrived' basket will look better than a half dead one, however, and you can use real plant material to create it.

Line the basket with moss (if you find it difficult to obtain at this time of year, use sprays of conifer foliage to provide a natural-looking lining), then fill it with a block of floral foam cut to size. If necessary use several small pieces.

Cut evergreen foliage and arrange in the basket to form an attractive ball-shape. Make sure you push plenty of pieces in the sides as well as the top, starting with the foliage. Then add shoots with berries, and to provide more colour use sprigs of flowers that will last a long time when cut. Heathers are ideal, but other flowers that you may find in the garden in late autumn include some of the mahonias and laurustinus (*Viburnum tinus*).

A basket like this will last for many weeks, and you can keep it looking attractive by replacing shoots that deteriorate. Remember to keep the floral foam moist.

Ordinary hanging baskets are not a practical proposition for late autumn and winter, as the compost tends to freeze solid and few plants will remain attractive. But you can use your baskets to display cut branches by filling it with floral foam (as used by flower arrangers), and inserting foliage and berries to form a ball of colour that will last for weeks and possibly months. This one contains Euonymus fortunei *'Emerald 'n' Gold' and 'Emerald Gaiety',* Elaeagnus pungens *'Maculata', Cape heather flowers and holly and pernettya berries.*

more exposed than tubs and troughs, and therefore more vulnerable to winds and cold air. It is better to keep the summer occupants flowering for as long as possible, by regular feeding and dead-heading, and then try planting a winter basket, rather than attempt to cram in an extra display for autumn. If you want to use your baskets for a little autumn and early winter colour, why not cheat and use the baskets for outdoor flower-arranging (see page 45)?

WINDOWBOXES AND TROUGHS

Once the summer flowers in a mixed container begin to fade, use a few autumn-flowering bulbs and dwarf shrubs to fill in the gaps. These will also bring a bit of extra colour to permanent mixed plantings.

Colchicums (the so-called autumn crocuses) will bring bold splashes of colour to a container just when it needs it. There are many species and varieties, and all those likely to be found in shops have large flowers like giant crocuses. They will even flower out of the soil, and unless you buy them promptly flower shoots may already be appearing (leaves do not appear until the spring). These really do bring 'instant' results, so use them wherever a container needs a bit of colour boost.

Some true crocuses flower in the autumn (see page 48); these are less spectacular but more useful for adding a little late colour to the base of a permanent tree or mixed planting. If you want them to boost colour among flagging bedding plants, the corms are best potted up in small pots as soon as available and plunged into a mixed planting when they are coming into flower.

Autumn is also a time for imagination and innovation when it comes to filling unexpected gaps. If an early frost has killed just one or two plants in a window-box, try filling the gaps with pot-plants like ornamental peppers and chrysanthemums.

Spring comes early

An autumn bulb box will make a truly unusual feature: it will look as though spring has arrived early. If you have a spare windowbox or trough they can be planted directly into this in later summer and grown on in an inconspicuous spot until the bulbs begin to bloom. As few of us have unfilled containers in late summer, bulbs can also be planted in small pots and plunged into the windowbox later, once the summer flowers have been cleared. Another advantage of growing them in pots is that you can plant extra bulbs to replace those that have finished flowering, so extending the season.

Skimmias make attractive plants for an autumn container and can be planted in the garden if you need the container for other plants in the spring. This is S. japonica *'Reevesiana', with* Erica gracilis, *a Cape heather, as a companion. The heather is not hardy and generally has to be discarded, but not until it has given many weeks of autumn and early winter colour.*

Good bulbs to try include: clochicums, *Crocus sativus*, *C. speciosus*, *C. zonatus* and *Sternbergia lutea*. If you are growing the bulbs in pots, plant flower of the west wind (*Zephyranthes*) too. These are usually sold in the spring, and species that you are likely to find are *Z. candida* and *Z. grandiflora*.

Bulbs are beautiful but brief in their flowering, and it is difficult to have everything in flower at once. This makes it difficult to achieve the overall impact that summer flowers create, with a mass of different kinds and lots of colour out all at once. Growing them in pots with plenty of spares to keep the rotation going as described above is one way of avoiding too many flat spots.

> Plant a trough with lots of young heathers coming into flower, and grow the bulbs between these. The heather flowers and foliage hold the arrangement together as the bulbs come and go ... and they can be planted in the garden afterwards.

Colourful chrysanthemums

By manipulating the amount of light they receive, professional growers induce pot chrysanthemums to flower throughout the year, and by treating them with growth-retarding chemicals they can keep them dwarf and compact. They are sold as houseplants, but bring instant colour to an autumn windowbox, and are tough enough to withstand the cold nights of autumn. Grow them alone or mix them with some compact foliage shrubs.

Korean chrysanthemums deserve to be grown more widely, and they are excellent for a large trough (some grow to about 60 cm (2 ft), which makes them rather tall for a windowbox), and come in all the usual chrysanthemum colours. Grow them in 20 cm (10 in) pots during the summer then use them to replace summer bedding in the autumn.

Year-round pot chrysanthemums are usually discarded when they have finished flowering, but they can sometimes be grown as garden plants afterwards. Pot them up and keep them in a cool greenhouse or cold frame for the winter, being careful not to over-water, then plant out in the spring. Some may survive and flower as much taller garden plants the following autumn, and even into early winter. It is a gamble as many different kinds are used for year-round production and not all will take to the garden afterwards.

Autumn tints

Autumn tints, which are associated with deciduous trees and shrubs, sound an unlikely option for a windowbox or tub. With a little imagination, however, you can enjoy some really attractive foliage effects ... and by choosing appropriate plants the effect will last for weeks rather than days.

The hardy plumbago (*Ceratostigma willmottianum*) is a semi-woody plant that grows to about 75 cm (2½ ft) in the garden, but young plants in containers are unlikely to be more than about half this height. The leaves turn purplish-red in autumn and remain like this for weeks. Blue flowers continue to appear among them through to mid and late autumn.

You need nothing else in the container, but if the trough or windowbox is large or if you prefer a mixed planting, a few small plants of the herringbone cotoneaster (*C. horizontalis*) planted so that they tumble over the front of the container are unlikely to disappoint. The leaves turn orange before falling, and although this can happen quickly after a sharp frost the cheerful red berries remain.

Young specimens of many of the berrying shrubs suggested for tubs (see pages 50–1) would also be suitable for a large trough. Buy these in pots from a garden centre – their cost is easily justified because these highly desirable plants can be used in the garden afterwards.

Cape heathers and cabbages

Cape heathers (*Erica hyemalis* and *E. gracilis*), which are usually on sale by mid autumn, make long-lasting plants for an autumn windowbox or tub. They are sold as pot-plants so they are already showy (ordinary garden heathers bought as young plants lack impact). They are not hardy enough to grow in the garden, but will flower for weeks, and even then the spikes of dead flowers remain quite attractive. Discard them when the time comes for them to make way for something else.

Cabbages and kales sound as though they belong in the kitchen garden rather than in windowboxes, but keep an open mind. There are attractive ornamental forms of both vegetables, which are almost as colourful as flowers and a lot longer lasting than most blooms at this time of year. Purples and pinks are the main colours, but some are white – an excellent choice for a dull porch, where they bring brightness on the most cheerless day.

There is one problem with cabbages and kales: they have a stiff, formal outline that makes them look too regimented on their own. Incorporate them with other plants. Foliage plants can be as effective as flowers for this, but try mixing white ornamental cabbages with the pinks and purples of Cape heathers – a happy association that will bring colour to a porch for months in late autumn and even into early winter.

The autumn glory of hebes

Hebes are a contradiction. They are not dependably hardy except in very mild districts (they may survive several winters only to be lost in a severe one), yet some of them will bloom into late autumn and even into winter. If you live in a reasonably mild area splash out on a selection of late-flowering hebes, using them in troughs and windowboxes for the first autumn, then plant them in the garden. You could use variegated hebes for contrast, but rather than risk too much investment in hebes that you might lose, choose something hardy and winter-dependable: try mixing them with an evergreen foliage shrub such as *Euonymus fortunei* 'Emerald 'n' Gold' or 'Emerald Gaiety'. Hebes to look for are

'Autumn Glory', 'Great Orme', 'Marjorie', and 'Midsummer Beauty'. Some eventually make substantial shrubs in the garden, but the young plants sold in garden centres are suitable for containers. Make sure they have some flowers when you buy for a windowbox or trough display.

TUBS

Many of the plant combinations suggested for troughs can be used in tubs, perhaps around a tall plant such as a sweet bay as a centrepiece to provide height. Bring some seasonal colour to permanent occupants such as deciduous trees and collections of dwarf conifers by planting clumps of crocuses and colchicums.

Potty about nerines

Nerines seem determined to make autumn bright and beautiful. The large heads of spidery-looking pink flowers bloom and bloom, and in a mild autumn seem reluctant to give up until winter arrives. Their pale, bright colouring, which is not masked by leaves as the foliage appears in spring, creates the sort of display that will take the eye across the garden.

There is a price to pay for such a splendid spectacle. The bulbs, which should be planted in spring, are not cheap . . . and they require a season or two to settle down to really prolific blooming. They resent disturbance, and the container will be bare for most of summer, so plant them in a large pot or tub (about 30 cm (12 in) diameter) light enough to move around. Keep it in a sunny spot during spring and summer and move it to a position of prominence once the flowers appear. Overwinter the pot in a cold or cool greenhouse (or even a porch) in cold areas.

A pernettya pot

Pernettyas are unspectacular shrubs for most of the year, with insignificant flowers and unimpressive foliage. Their moment of glory comes as autumn approaches and the large, luscious-looking berries, in shades of red, pink and white appear studded along the shoots.

You can buy small plants trained as standards, and these make an attractive centrepiece for a tub or large decorative pot. Plant small bush forms around the base, using the same variety for a co-ordinated approach, or in a contrasting colour.

Plant a suitable mate if you want to ensure a good crop of berries on your pernettyas. You need a male form of the plant to ensure good pollination. If keeping the plants in their container permanently (advisable if you have a chalky soil, as pernettyas need an acid soil), make sure you put the container near a male plant in the garden border when they are in flower.

Berried treasures

Many of the berrying plants described in the next chapter already have their colourful fruits by the autumn. Some, such as *Cotoneaster conspicuus* 'Decorus' will soon need a large tub, but others are naturally dwarf or very slow-growing and could be used to bring a bright splash of colour to a mixed planting or even to a smaller container such as a trough or windowbox. Look for *Gaultheria procumbens*, prostrate cotoneasters and *Vaccineum vitis-idaea*.

JOBS FOR AUTUMN

Autumn is a busy time for container gardeners, with old plants to discard, new ones to plant, and things to propagate for next year. Although demanding tasks such as frequent watering and feeding become less onerous, there are plenty of jobs to be done to maintain year round interest.

- **Take cuttings of pelargoniums (geraniums), fuchsias and other tender perennials** (including marguerites) in early autumn to overwinter in a greenhouse or conservatory. If suitable facilities for overwintering the cuttings are not available, try to overwinter the plants in a frost-free place, such as a cool but light bedroom, or even a protected porch, and take cuttings in spring.

Pernettyas are often sold as small plants already laden with autumn berries. This container has one trained as a small standard for a centrepiece, with several smaller bush forms around the edge. The berries contrast well with the Elaeagnus pungens *'Maculata' in the background.*

- **Bring tender plants indoors** or into a greenhouse before the nights get cold.

- **Plant colchicums** and any other available autumn-flowering bulbs as soon as possible in early autumn.

- **Plant spring-flowering bulbs and biennials** such as wallflowers and double daisies in mid or late autumn. Bulbs should be planted at varying depths according to variety, and not spaced too far apart (Fig. 4).

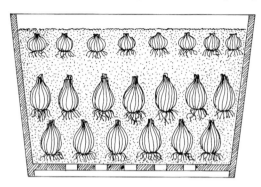

Fig 4 *For a bold display pack as many bulbs as possible into a large tub or trough. Place one layer of large bulbs such as daffodils low down, close but not touching, then add more compost and plant another row between the noses of those in the first layer. Plant small bulbs above if appropriate.*

- **Protect vulnerable shrubs** by late autumn, before the very cold weather. See page 109 for advice on how to do this.

- **Protect containers that are not frost-proof**. By late autumn terracotta pots that are not frost-proof should be taken into a greenhouse or conservatory if they contain perennial plants, or emptied and stored in a dry place.

- **Plant containers for winter interest**. See next chapter for suggestions.

- **Plan and plant containers for year-round interest**. If possible plant them in early autumn so that the plants become established before the winter.

POT THEM TO PACK THEM

Reserve crocuses, dwarf narcissi, hyacinths, scillas, snowdrops and dwarf irises, potted up now can be used for improvised displays next spring. You can then use them to brighten up containers that seem to lack impact, or make up pretty arrangements in baskets and other unusual containers that might be damaged if you attempt to grow the bulbs in them all through the winter. Line the basket or container with polythene, remove the bulbs from their pots, and pack them in firmly with peat, then cover the surface with moss or chipped bark, for an instant and inspirational arrangement.

CHAPTER 4

WINTER INTEREST

WINTER IS THE real challenge of year-round container gardening. How successful you are in meeting it depends on where you live and on your imagination.

Some suggestions in this chapter can be followed closely, others are only guidelines to be adapted to your own tastes and local conditions. If you live in an exceptionally cold area it may be necessary to substitute tougher plants for some of those mentioned. Elsewhere, where the winters are exceptionally mild the choice of shrubs is wider (hebes, for instance, have not been recommended, but in very favourable areas they are particularly useful).

Many of the permanent plantings in Chapter 5 also provide pockets of interest and help to form a backdrop against which to add seasonal colour. Be generous with the use of variegated evergreen foliage, and rather than dot your containers around the garden in places seldom explored in the cold days of winter, group them together where you can appreciate them. Suitable positions include an open porch, a sheltered corner in the front garden that is seen as visitors approach the door, or on the patio near French windows or patio doors where they can be appreciated from the warmth and comfort of indoors.

WINDOWBOXES AND TROUGHS

Windowboxes and troughs planted with spring bulbs can be improved with a few winter-flowering pansies to combat the bleakness of bare compost while bulbs are emerging. Invaluable though they are, winter-flowering pansies are unlikely to flower well until late winter and early spring, but they will produce a few flowers throughout the winter whenever there is a reasonably long mild spell. Bushier, leafy plants like forget-me-nots are better at covering the surface with greenery but do not contribute winter colour.

Bulbous beauties

Winter-flowering bulbs are small and delicate-looking, so they are ideal for a windowbox where they are readily appreciated. Unfortunately flowering times are unpredictable so the likelihood of a collection of different types flowering together is not favourable. Overcome this by planting a collection of dwarf

Winter heathers can make a real focal point if artistically arranged as here. A small plant of Euonymus fortunei *'Emerald 'n' Gold' brings a dash of bright foliage.*

shrubs such as young winter-flowering heathers or *Euonymus fortunei* 'Emerald 'n' Gold' and 'Emerald Gaiety' as a backdrop and grow the bulbs in small 8–10 cm (3–4 in) pots. Grow as many different winter-flowering bulbs as you can find and afford in pots *exactly the same size*: plunge some straight into the compost in the trough or windowbox, and grow the rest on in a cold frame or cold greenhouse (otherwise a spare piece of ground in good light, but plunge the pots in the soil for a little extra protection). As the flowers come into bloom, remove the existing pots in the arrangement and insert the new ones. By rotating them like this, brave winter-flowering blooms can be sustained over a long period, and the background planting ensures that the windowbox never looks bare.

Bulbs to plant for a succession of winter bloom include *Anemone blanda*, *Crocus laevigatus*, *C. tommasinianus*, *Cyclamen coum*, *Eranthis hyemalis* (winter aconite),

Galanthus caucasicus (a snowdrop), *Iris danfordiae*, *Narcissus cyclamineus* 'February Gold' and 'Peeping Tom'. These are all readily available, but there are plenty of more obscure, early-flowering species if you are prepared to search the catalogues of bulb specialists.

Winter into spring can be a natural progression with the kind of bulb box described. Plant more pots of early spring bulbs, such as *Crocus chrysanthus*, *Galanthus nivalis* (common snowdrop), *Iris reticulata* and *Narcissus* 'Tête-à-Tête'. Then for later spring plant chionodoxas and dwarf scillas. Be sure to use the same-sized pots as those for the winter-flowerers. By simply slotting in fresh pots of bulbs as they bloom you will ensure a continuity of interest from mid winter through to mid spring, by which time the more traditional spring displays take over.

DON'T DISTURB

First-year flowering can be disappointing with those bulbs, corms and tubers that take a year or two to become established. Winter aconites, *Anemone blanda* and even snowdrops can look sparse for the first season. Make them look like an established clump by planting close together in the pots. After flowering, plunge the pots in a spare piece of ground where they can die down naturally. Lift the pot again next year for an even better display.

Flowers, foliage and fruit

Dwarf shrubs provide the best chance of a continuous display, but they look best in troughs or large windowboxes; in a small windowbox they can look out of proportion. Where the container is to be viewed from a low angle (eye-level boxes, for instance) plant a low carpeter like one of the *Euonymus fortunei* varieties or ivies, to mask the base.

Where there is space, combine a winter heather for flowers with a berried plant, a skimmia with attractive red flower buds, such as *S. japonica* 'Rubella' and a bright variegated foliage plant such as *Aucuba japonica* 'Crotonifolia'. If space is limited, settle for just two of them, but plant a couple of each.

Alpine landscapes

Try making a mini rock garden in a spare windowbox or trough. The results will be more convincing if the container is large. Do not attempt to create the kind of planting effect needed for a sink garden in a container purely for winter interest. Place the emphasis on textures and shapes.

The plants will be for winter show only, so the old compost can be left in the container. Transfer the plants to the garden when you need the container for a summer display.

Possible plants are suggested below, but for this kind of display you can often raid the rock garden, or use cuttings and small plants that you have propagated. If you have houseleeks (sempervivums) growing over a small stone, borrow stone and houseleeks together to give the arrangement a sense of instant maturity. It may be necessary to buy a few alpines from the garden centre to supplement those from your own garden.

The success of this type of container depends on how creatively you arrange the plants. Incorporate some small pieces of rock and cover the surface with crushed stone or stone chippings.

Choose evergreens with a distinctive shape or a strong and positive outline, such as houseleeks (sempervivums), thrift (armeria), alpine dianthus, *Oxalis adenophylla*, rock saxifrages, *Sedum spathulifolium* 'Cape Blanco' and 'Purpureum', and thymes – *Thymus* 'Doone Valley' (gold-variegated) and *T. × citriodorus* 'Silver Posie' (also sold as 'Variegatus') are good ones. Add a couple of very small conifers if you can find them – the species or variety is unimportant for this temporary display, just choose very small plants or young cuttings with an attractive shape (young specimens will also be cheaper).

TUBS

Bulbs suggested for windowboxes can be used around the base of deciduous trees and shrubs, but continuity of bloom is less important than a bold splash of flowers at one time, so choose just one or two types and plant them directly into the compost in the container. Evergreen permanent plantings (see Chapter 5) provide background interest but plant one or two winter-interest shrubs as specimens that can be moved into a place of prominence at this time.

Winter-flowering shrubs

Winter-flowering shrubs do not add much to the summer scene, and the deciduous ones are uninspiring for most of winter too! A few bulbs around the base, or a carpet of winter pansies, will overcome this shortcoming, and use summer bedding around the base to justify the space the containers take up in summer.

Choose just one or two choice winter-flowering shrubs to grow as large specimens that will become real focal points during the bleakest months of the year. Wintersweet (*Chimonanthus fragrans*) and witch hazel (*Hamamelis mollis*) will eventually make quite substantial shrubs; they need a large container to grow happily. Both have distinctive yellow flowers in winter.

Evergreens, which have something good to contribute for the whole year, are a better bet where space or money is limited. *Mahonia* 'Charity' is an imposing evergreen with large leaves and an upright habit that brings a touch of distinction to a patio throughout the year. The clusters of bright yellow, scented flowers start to open as early as mid autumn, and are still bringing cheer to the garden in early winter. The upright habit makes it practical to plant a compact evergreen, such as *Pachysandra terminalis* 'Variegata', around the base. Laurustinus (*Viburnum tinus*) bears its clusters of small white or pink flowers from autumn through until spring, set against attractive evergreen leaves. Laurustinus makes a shapely bush that you can clip to a formal outline – try a pair either side of your door instead of bay if you live in a cold area.

BRIGHT BUT BRIEF

Florists' cyclamen (*C. persicum*), *Primula obconica*, cinerarias, and pot azaleas are among the plants sometimes used to bring bloom and cheer in the depths of winter. All these bring much-needed colour whenever the weather is not too severe, but at a price . . . they may last in good condition for just days or a couple of weeks then have to be discarded. Use them if you are prepared to regard them as you would bunches of cut flowers for the home: beautiful while they last but transient, to be replaced frequently.

Some tender pot-plants can be used with more confidence. Winter cherries (*Solanum* spp.) and ornamental peppers (*Capsicum annuum*) hold their fruits for many weeks unless the weather is exceptionally severe. The foliage may drop, but the fruits remain decorative, so plant them among small hardy evergreen shrubs such as heathers or hebes.

Hellebores and elephants' ears

Herbaceous plants do not always come to mind for winter interest, yet there are evergreen herbaceous plants (they retain winter foliage but are not woody like a shrub) to bring a very special charm to the winter garden.

The Christmas rose (*Helleborus niger*) really can be enjoyed in flower at Christmas, and is followed by the Lenten rose (*H. orientalis*) in late winter and early spring. You can have even more hellebores in flower if you include the deciduous *H. atrorubens* (mid winter to mid spring) and green-flowered *H. viridis* (late winter and early spring). Grow a collection of these in a large container, and leave them undisturbed. Do not expect many flowers the first year, but subsequently they will be highly prized members of your container plant collection.

In containers that are large enough, such as a half-barrel, plant hellebores and the ground-covering bergenias (elephants' ears). These have pretty flowers in spring (usually pink, but sometimes white or red), and a variety such as B. 'Ballawley' has foliage that turns attractive shades of red and purple in cold weather. These plants are also useful as an underplanting for shrubs in containers.

Algerian irises

The Algerian iris (*I. unguicularis*, sometimes still sold as *I. stylosa*) is an evergreen herbaceous plant with blue typically iris-shaped flowers that nestle among the foliage from mid autumn to early spring, though in some years blooming does not start in earnest until late winter; it benefits from a really hot dry summer. This is a gem that deserves to be grown on its own and allowed to form a large clump. It flowers best if given a season or two to settle down. For a happy association, place the container in front of yellow winter jasmine (*Jasminum nudiflorum*).

By choosing evergreen herbaceous plants carefully you can plant up a year-round container that will still look good at the dullest time of year. This trough was photographed in the depths of winter – the plants are hellebores, Carex morrowii *'Evergold',* Euphorbia amygdaloides *'Purpurea' and* Ajuga reptans *'Catlin's Giant'.*

Heathers and berries

The hardy winter-flowering heathers (*Erica carnea* and *E. × darleyensis*) can be disappointing in containers, but they are worth trying if you mix them with a slightly taller shrub that will help to give the container a bit more height and contrast. The Cape heathers (which are not hardy) can also be used, although they will have to be discarded later.

Small skimmias make a good centrepiece for winter heathers, and *S. japonica reevesiana* can usually be bought in the autumn already laden with clusters of red berries.

Hollies are associated with winter, but a large specimen is a focal point at any time. A standard looks really impressive, but takes years to train. Try clipping them to a simple pyramid if 'lollipop' standards are too daunting to train. Unfortunately hollies are slow-growing, and berries are unlikely to be produced on very young plants. (Choose a female variety, and check whether it needs a mate.)

Ideas from autumn

Some of the suggestions for autumn tubs, such as the pernettya pot (page 50), will remain attractive into early winter, and in mild areas the hebe arrangements will still be producing a few flowers. Make the most of berried plants, as some retain their fruits until mid winter if birds are not a problem.

Skimmias and Cape heathers are useful plants to bridge the gap between late autumn and early winter. Use them to add a bit of late colour to a permanent planting of conifers or other evergreens.

Winter hanging baskets are seldom successful except in large cities where they are often protected from very severe weather by the buildings and the 'heat island' effect, but the fun basket of foliage and berries suggested on page 45 works just as well in winter, and it makes an attractive porch decoration at Christmas, especially if you include holly and ivy among the plants.

JOBS FOR WINTER

Early winter is mainly a time for planning, for studying seed and nursery catalogues in the comfort of the armchair, and perhaps gleaning a few useful ideas from books that can be developed into something that is right for you and your garden. By late winter seeds and plants should have been ordered, and some seed-sowing will already be under way.

- **Order catalogues**. Seed catalogues are invaluable as a source of inspiration and as a planning aid. Although a huge range of suitable plants can be bought from garden centres in late spring, raising your own seedlings opens up new horizons . . . a much wider choice of varieties and colours, the chance to try something very new or interestingly different, and the sheer satisfaction of raising your own plants. It is now possible to order seedlings and young plants from some seed companies – ideal if you lack a greenhouse or conservatory to start them off in, though the range of plants available is obviously limited.

Some companies offer collections of plants (not seeds) for hanging baskets and other containers. These are well worth considering, even if you use the plants in arrangements different from the combination suggested in the catalogue.

For the more exotic plants, like daturas and even bananas, you need to obtain lists from nurseries specializing in tender plants. Some bulb merchants offer plants of exotics suitable for patio containers.

- **Order seeds and plants**. Do not overlook bulbs. Not only summer-flowering types such as pendulous begonias and patio-sized dahlias, but autumn-flowering gems like nerines and zephyranthes.

- **Sow geraniums (pelargoniums) and fibrous-rooted begonias,** and other plants that need a lengthy growing period before they flower (Fig. 5). If you have a light place and warmth in which to grow them on, sow in mid winter, otherwise wait until late winter.

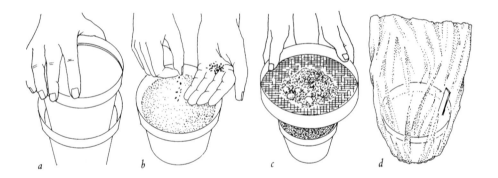

Fig 5 *Even without a greenhouse it is easy to raise a few seedlings for your containers. This is especially worthwhile if you want to try varieties that are not readily available as plants.*

*If raising plants on a windowsill, sow in pots to save space. Use a seed compost and level it with the base of another pot (**a**) before sprinkling the seeds thinly and carefully (**b**). Cover the seeds with compost (**c**) unless the packet advises otherwise. Label then cover with a sheet of glass or a polythene bag (**d**). Keep in a warm place and be sure to give the seedlings plenty of light once they emerge. Pot up into individual pots when the seedlings are large enough to handle.*

- **Take cuttings of tender perennials in late winter**. If cuttings were not taken last autumn, start geraniums, fuchsias and tender perennials such as marguerites into growth in mid or late winter, then take cuttings from the new shoots.

- **Check that winter protection is satisfactory** on vulnerable plants left outdoors.

- **Check winter and spring containers** and remove any dead or diseased leaves and premature flower buds.

CHAPTER 5

PERMANENT PLANTINGS

MOST CONTAINERS ARE planted for immediate if rather transient impact. Permanently planted containers are less colourful and take longer to look established, but most compensate by being well clothed whatever the season. That does not mean they are dull, and by adding a few colourful seasonal plants even collections of evergreens will be far from boring.

Many plants mentioned in this chapter grow large in time. Small specimens can often be used in mixed containers, but if you buy a large one or you lift a well established specimen from the garden, pot them up individually. By careful juxtaposition of several plants with different shapes, colours and textures, a similar effect to a mixed container can be achieved. If you get fed up with the effect, just move them around to create another one.

Individual plants can be changed occasionally, and large specimen trees and shrubs may eventually have to be moved to a bigger container, but most remain in the same container and the same compost for several years. This demands a good loam-based compost. Peat composts lack the weight and anchorage qualities of a loam compost, necessary for large shrubs and small trees, and they become impoverished more readily.

Do not be tempted to use garden soil because a large container requires a lot of compost. Long-term container plants need a good start in life and a compost has to retain nutrients and release them slowly over a long period.

Choose a container that allows for growth, and plant in a good loam-based compost such as John Innes No. 3.

WINDOWBOXES

Windowboxes are more challenging than troughs and tubs. With few exceptions they hold less compost, and the proportions seem inappropriate for most shrubby plants and conifers. They are also less easy to protect in winter. Most of us expect windowboxes to be brimming with colour, with bushy bedding plants and brilliant trailers, an effect difficult to achieve with a permanent planting. Shrubs and evergreen herbaceous plants provide gentler, more restrained beauty, without any of the more frenetic changing of plants every few months that seasonal windowboxes require.

Purely hebes

Hebes are happiest in areas where winters are mild. In a very cold area, take the box down in the autumn and put it in a greenhouse or even a protected porch. They do not require heat, just protection from very severe cold.

Try a hebes only box, but combine foliage effect with flowers. Two of the finest variegated hebes for a container are *H. × franciscana* 'Variegata' and *H. × andersonii* 'Variegata'. With time the latter makes a much taller shrub in a border, but young plants in a container are very similar; both are grown primarily for their creamy white and green leaves, and each has the bonus of pretty blue flowers. Use either of these with other small, dome-shaped hebes such as *H. rakaiensis* (pale green leaves and white flowers in early and mid summer) and *H.* 'Red Edge' (leaves flushed red at the margins). Use these three plants for the main grouping, then if the box is large enough for a couple of extra plants at the front use the grey-leaved *H. pinguifolia* 'Pagei', which has a prostrate habit and will be happy to tumble over the front of the box.

A cactus garden

Cacti sound unlikely occupants of a windowbox, but they make a pretty and interesting box for the patio wall or beneath a window where you do not feel obliged to plant a prolific and floriferous box to be appreciated from a distance. Make a seasonal cactus garden by plunging small cacti in pots into the window-box, or plant it on a permanent basis but take it indoors for the winter.

The cacti chosen are less important than how they are arranged. Choose varied and interesting shapes, some tall and narrow ones, others round and squat, a few with flat pads like the opuntias. You can often buy small cacti in flower and these add even more interest. Make the effect more convincing by placing a thick layer of fine stone chippings over the surface and, if you can manage it, incorporate a few very small rocks too.

This is one windowbox that you can go away and leave for a week without worrying about watering!

Alpine appeal

Alpines can be grown very successfully in windowboxes. Paint bold rivers of gold between islands of blue and purple in spring simply by mixing the yellow *Alyssum saxatile* and various aubrietas. If this sounds too vulgar and rampant, grow a collection of choice, well-behaved alpines and plant the windowbox as you would a sink garden, and finish it with an attractive stone chipping mulch. If a particular group of alpines appeals grow a collection of these – houseleeks (sempervivums) are an excellent choice because they are neat and restrained, there are lots of different shapes, sizes and colours, they are evergreen, and there is a bonus of quite attractive flowers in summer.

Opposite: *This trained bay tree is the kind of feature that is sure to attract attention. Although this kind of training is beyond the scope of most amateurs, the principle of a simple but striking trained plant set against a plain painted wall is one that is easy to adapt.*

An alpine box is much less demanding to look after than one containing seasonal bedding, and succulent kinds like houseleeks will look after themselves at holiday times. As with a cactus box, it needs careful siting.

Happy with herbaceous

Most border perennials are unwilling occupants of a container if you treat them as transient plants for a season, but those with a suitably compact habit often perform well if allowed to grow undisturbed for a couple of seasons.

Very dwarf hostas are useful for a shady position if you can tolerate bare boxes in winter. Hosta roots form an impenetrable mass so inter-planting them with winter-interest bulbs is seldom satisfactory.

For all-season interest, combine charmers like the yellowish-green lady's mantle (*Alchemilla mollis*) with blue *Campanula carpatica*, compact and fragrant pinks like *Dianthus* 'Doris', the purple-black grass-like evergreen *Ophiopogon planiscapus nigrescens* and carpeting *Ajuga reptans*. The ajuga comes in many colour forms, most are attractively variegated, and the leaves persist for most of the year. If the box is not large enough to accommodate all these, try a combination of dianthus (greyish leaves) with the ophiopogon (almost black foliage), both of which are evergreen. Use the ajuga as a carpet between them, or introduce some yellow Bowles' golden grass (*Milium effusum aureum*).

This kind of herbaceous windowbox is generally best in its second and third years, then requires replanting.

Black, grey and gold

Combine the almost black *Ophiopogon planiscapus nigrescens* with the cream and green *O. jaburan* 'Variegatus', both of which are evergreen and have grass-like leaves and seldom grow more than about 23 cm (9 in) tall. Add a few plants of the gold-variegated rush *Acorus gramineus* 'Wogon', and some grey-leaved dianthus such as 'Doris', with its pretty pink flowers if you want flowers and a touch of fragrance.

The multicoloured chameleon

Houttuynia cordata 'Chameleon' is so bright that flowers are unnecessary. It has small white flowers, but they are insignificant in comparison with the multicoloured foliage, which is a patchwork of yellow, green, bronze and red. Plant a couple of windowboxes with nothing else . . . and perhaps grow a pot of it beneath them for a study in co-ordination. The next year it will look better still, and when it needs dividing you will have no problem in finding new homes for the offspring.

This is an herbaceous plant that dies back – the only drawback – so you will want to store the containers in a spare corner for the winter.

Conifer composition

Use a few young dwarf conifers to provide a framework against which to plant small seasonal bulbs to provide a changing scene. A small windowbox will have room for perhaps three conifers (the golden *Thuja occidentalis* 'Rheingold' flanked by a pair of green *Juniperus communis* 'Compressa'), in front of which you can plant small bulbs to flower in spring and autumn (spring and autumn crocuses, snowdrops for spring, *Sternbergia lutea* for autumn, for example), and small-leaved variegated ivy to trail down the front.

Garden centres have a huge choice of dwarf conifers, often available as small specimens. After a few years they may outgrow the windowbox, but give them a new lease of life in the garden or even in shrub tubs or troughs where they have more space to develop.

TUBS AND TROUGHS

Troughs are usually larger than windowboxes, so they offer more scope with the opportunity to use larger plants. Their extra size generally means extra weight to move, so whenever possible use plants that remain interesting through the seasons.

Large pots, tubs, and other large containers such as half-barrels offer enormous scope for year-round planting. Plastic shrub tubs, square as well as round, are inexpensive and will usually accommodate perhaps three small or medium-sized shrubs along with a few bulbs or pansies as fillers if things look bare at the base.

PLAN FOR SUCCESSION

This is especially important for permanently planted containers. Plant early spring bulbs around a deciduous tree, mix some deciduous shrubs in among the evergreens to prevent the arrangement becoming too predictable and boring – or use some evergreens that have flowers or berries to introduce an element of change.

Flowers and foliage

Shrubs with pretty flowers often lack attractive foliage and vice versa. This is not a problem in a shrub border where there is space to grow many different kinds, some of which will always provide cover or interest at a particular time. In containers every occupant has to earn its space.

A good container shrub has attractive flowers *and* foliage . . . and ideally a neat shape too. Here are some candidates that qualify (if, in due course, they outgrow even a large tub, they can be planted out in the garden):

Laurustinus (*Viburnum tinus*) has neat evergreen foliage and a tidy shape that lends itself to formal shaping. The white or pink flowers start in autumn and continue till spring.

Snowy mespilus (*Amelanchier canadensis* and *A. lamarckii*) is covered with white flowers in mid spring, followed by crimson fruits that ripen to black by early summer . . . and there is a bonus of attractive autumn tints before the leaves fall.

Camellias have to be near the top of any list of flowering evergreens: large, almost rose-like flowers in spring, in shades of pink, red and white, set against attractive glossy green leaves. Choose a hardy variety such as one of the *C. × williamsii* or *C. japonica* hybrids if you cannot give it shelter in severe weather.

The hardy plumbago (*Ceratostigma willmottianum*) is almost herbaceous in appearance, making a compact shrub that is ideal for containers. The blue flowers appear in mid summer and are still putting in an appearance in late autumn, when the foliage takes on beautiful autumn tints. It, too, may appreciate a little shelter, especially when young.

Heathers are best known for their flowers, but let coloured foliage varieties charm you in a different way. Some of the *Erica* and many of the *Calluna* varieties come in beautiful shades of silver, gold and russet, the colours often intensifying in cold weather. Mahonias, too, are grown mainly for floral effect, but their large spiky evergreen leaves make a bold statement and provide a feature throughout the year.

The compact cotton lavender (*Santolina chamaecyparissus*) and the larger *Senecio* 'Sunshine', on the other hand, are two grey-leaved shrubs grown primarily for foliage effect, but their cheerful yellow flowers are a bonus that is far from a marginal benefit.

Cacti and succulents can make an appealing feature if arranged in the form of a small 'garden'. But make sure it is light enough to be carried indoors for the winter. This one contains echeverias, sedums, an aloe and stapelia.

The stately yuccas are admired most when the huge spikes of nodding white bells tower above the rosette-like cluster of sword-shaped leaves. If you grow a variegated one such as *Y. filamentosa* 'Variegata' or *Y. gloriosa* 'Variegata' the foliage will be a feature too.

Choisya ternata, the so-called Mexican orange blossom, is worth growing in its green form, with fragrant white flowers beautifully framed by the pleasing evergreen foliage. Even better for year-round appeal is the golden form, 'Sundance'.

Contrasting colours

Group plants to make the most of contrasting colours as well as shapes, whether planting several small ones in a single container or larger specimens in individual containers.

Try a purple or reddish phormium (spiky leaves) with a green- and cream-variegated hebe such as *H.* × *franciscana* 'Variegata' (neat, rounded shape) and a grey-leaved curry plant (*Helichrysum angustifolium*), which has a feathery outline.

Grow the purple-leaved sage in front of the golden *Choisya ternata* 'Sundance', and if you have room for a third plant use one of the silver-leaved artemisias.

Some ideas for dwarf conifer combinations using shapes as counterpoint are suggested on page 65, but contrast colours too: *Juniperus squamata* 'Blue Star'

Sempervivums are ideal container plants. They come in many different forms and almost thrive on neglect. Used to dry conditions, they will not object if you take a holiday and forget to water them.

('blue', spreading) with *Thuja orientalis* 'Aurea Nana' (yellow, oval) and *Taxus baccata* 'Fastigiata Robusta' (very dark green, narrow pillar) make a trio that is packed with colour contrasts as well as varied profiles.

Feature foliage

Foliage plays an important role in permanent plantings, as a foil for flowers and to provide year-round interest. If you depend on container plants to provide stimulation and interest every month of the year, on a balcony garden or a patio overlooked by the living room for example, then think of painting with foliage as well as flowers.

Variegated plants and those with gold or grey leaves prevent greens being boring but leaf size and shape provide necessary contrasts. Many large-leaved plants help to create a 'designer' feel for a patio. Other shrubs sustain foliage interest by changing colour. *Pieris formosa forrestii* is a handsome evergreen with brilliant red young growths, and a bonus of slightly fragrant white flowers in mid spring. It needs an ericaceous compost, but *Photinia × fraseri* 'Red Robin' has similar brilliant red young foliage without the need for a special acid compost.

The stag's horn sumach (*Rhus typhina*) makes a real focal point in a large tub. The large, divided leaves are held proudly as if the plant wants to show them off, and before they fall there is a real display of fireworks with orange and red autumn tints. The foliage is usually held well above the base, which is often bare, so plant some spring or winter bulbs around the base with ivies to cascade over the edge of the container.

Silver and gold

Use gold-leaved plants and those with bright yellow variegation to bring light to a dull corner. Or add a few dwarf shrubs with yellow-variegated leaves in a mixed planting to light up the base – a carpet of *Euonymus fortunei* 'Emerald 'n' Gold' is much more acceptable than bare compost, or even a mulch or bark chippings or gravel.

Golden or yellow-variegated shrubs that make imposing specimens in individual tubs include *Elaeagnus pungens* 'Maculata', *Euonymus japonicus* 'Aureopictus', *Choisya ternata* 'Sundance', and *Ilex crenata* 'Golden Gem', a dwarf, non-prickly, golden holly.

Silver and grey foliage and variegation bring more subtle qualities, but help to counterbalance the more fiery reds and bright yellows, while at the same time relieving the dullness of an all-green grouping.

Senecio 'Sunshine', with felted grey leaves and bright yellow daisy flowers, is best grown in a container on its own but use it to bring foliage contrast by placing it in front of dark evergreens or among a group of containers with bright or brash flowers.

Cotton lavender (*Santolina chamaecyparissus*) and some of the shrubby and herbaceous artemisias are compact enough to use in the same container as other foliage or flowering shrubs. *Helichrysum petiolare* is popular where a grey-leaved shrub with a cascading habit is required, but it is not hardy enough to form part of a permanent planting.

INVEST IN SOME IVIES

Ivies are practical rather than pretty plants, real workhorses among container plants. They can be used as feature plants, but more usually form a kind of ground cover in permanently planted tubs and troughs, covering the compost and dripping over the edges of the container to give it a really well-clothed appearance. Ivies are particularly useful for a shady spot where flowering trailers and cascaders do not perform so well. They can also be left in place more or less permanently in windowboxes and troughs that are replanted with seasonal plants a couple of times a year, but choose small-leaved varieties and be prepared to give them a haircut if they begin to outgrow their space.

Some of the most suitable with either gold or silver variegation are: 'Adam' (white-edged), 'Buttercup' (deep yellow), 'Glacier' (grey and green) and 'Goldheart' (splashed yellow).

Focal point plants

Bring a touch of distinction to your patio or courtyard with a few specimen shrubs that will bring an 'architectural' quality to the garden – plants with a distinctive and shapely profile that become focal points. Usually they have large or bold leaves, often held elegantly or aggressively.

Two of the most popular are *Fatsia japonica* and *Yucca filamentosa*. The fatsia, popularly called the false castor oil plant, not only has large hand-shaped leaves but in late autumn is often crowned with unusual ball-like heads of creamy white flowers. Yuccas are grown mainly for the huge flower spikes of white nodding bells, but the sword-like upward-pointing leaves provide a striking profile throughout the year.

The angelica tree (*Aralia elata*) is a tree with large, handsome leaves up to 1.5 m (5 ft) long that give the garden a lush, tropical touch. There are two very attractive variegated forms: 'Aureovariegata' (yellow leaf margins) and 'Variegata' (creamy white variegation). In warm climates they grow into quite tall trees, but in cooler parts and in containers they can be kept as a large shrub with suckers being produced from the base of the plant.

The Chusan or fan palm (*Trachycarpus fortunei*) is an evergreen palm with large fan-shaped leaves, hardy enough to grow outside in all but the coldest districts. It is more vulnerable in containers, so protect it well in winter (see page 109) or move it into a conservatory.

Gunnera manicata is one of the giants of the plant world, with huge, rough, rhubarb-like leaves. It is normally associated with bog and water gardens, but it can be grown in a large container such as a half-barrel provided it is kept very well watered. Leave the clump undisturbed for as long as possible, and protect the crown and container in winter.

Fancy and formal

A totally different effect can be achieved by using lots of formal shapes and shrubs clipped into pyramids, 'lollipops' and spirals. These are ideal for a courtyard garden, but look great on a modern patio too. Use a matching pair to frame the front door.

The most widely used plants are sweet bay (*Laurus nobilis*), and box (*Buxus sempervirens*), but hollies also make good trained and shaped shrubs, though you need patience with such slow growers.

Conifer collections

Conifers are plants that most people either adore or avoid, but whatever your prejudices, try to use a few for the contrasts that they contribute. The vast majority are evergreen and come in many diverse shapes, from container-hugging carpeters to slender pencil-shaped plants that contribute height without being oppressive; there are yellows and gold, 'blues' and variegated kinds, as well as a multitude of different greens. Many have a naturally trimmed look, growing into pyramids, balls or cones. This great diversity of colour, shape and texture offers scope for almost endless permutations for the creative container gardener. The suggestions below are just a few combinations to stimulate ideas for other groupings. It is a good idea to mix, say, an upright, globe-shaped or oval conifer with a prostrate one, to give the grouping shape and form as well as colour contrasts.

Try *Chamaecyparis pisifera* 'Filifera Aurea' (whip-like branches, gold), *Juniperus* 'Skyrocket' (narrow column, green) and *Thuja orientalis* 'Aurea Nana' (globular, gold) together. Or *Juniperus horizontalis* 'Glauca' (a 'blue' ground hugger that will trail over the edge of the container) with *Thuja occidentalis* 'Rheingold' (gold, oval) and *Chamaecyparis communis* 'Sentinel' (narrow and upright, green).

Other useful conifers to include in groups or as individual specimens are *Chamaecyparis lawsoniana* 'Ellwoodii', *C. pisifera* 'Boulevard', *Juniperus × media* 'Mint Julep', and *J. × media* 'Blaauw'.

HEATHER COMPANIONS

Conifers and heathers are well known as good companions for the garden, and they make happy marriages in containers too. Try planting *Calluna vulgaris* 'Gold Flame' (golden foliage, pink flowers) around the base of *Chamaecyparis pisifera* 'Boulevard' or *Erica carnea* 'Foxhollow', with its bright gold foliage, around the striking 'blue' foliage of *Juniperus squamata* 'Blue Star'.

Opposite: *A miniature water garden makes a refreshingly different sort of container garden. Half-barrels are ideal.*

Trees for tubs

Trees are often the last plants that newcomers to container gardening think about. If the garden is small, perhaps only a backyard, balcony, roof garden or patio, trees do at first sight seem inappropriate. Fortunately they are always smaller and more compact in a container than they would be in the open ground, and you need a few tall plants to give a container garden that extra dimension.

Some can be grown in large pots (about 30 cm (12 in) is the minimum practical size), but as the trees grow they may need something larger, such as a half-barrel.

Crab apples and ornamental cherries are particularly beautiful in flower, and some of these can be grown in containers. *Malus floribunda* and *M. sargentii* are pretty flowering crabs. The flagpole cherry (*Prunus* 'Amanogawa') has narrow, upright growth, so it will not cast too much shade.

Small trees with bright or colourful foliage can be more effective than those with pretty flowers. If you have space, grow the grey-leaved, dome-shaped weeping pear (*Pyrus salicifolia* 'Pendula') and one of the most outstanding of all trees for foliage effect, the golden *Robinia pseudoacacia* 'Frisia'.

The Japanese maples (*Acer palmatum*) are slow-growing trees with a rounded shape and are often shrub-like. There are many varieties, of which 'Dissectum' and 'Dissectum Atropurpureum' are among the most popular for containers. These add a special touch of elegance to a patio.

Two small pendulous trees that are unlikely to outgrow their welcome are *Salix caprea* 'Pendula' (Kilmarnock willow) and *Cotoneaster* 'Hybridus Pendulus'. The latter has small white flowers on its pendulous branches in summer, but is grown primarily for the bright red autumn berries clustered along its long drooping shoots. These are both very small trees anyway, and in a container will grow no higher than many shrubs.

All these are deciduous, so plant colchicums around the base for autumn interest and spring-flowering bulbs to bring early colour. Leave them undisturbed to form well-established clumps.

Rich and exotic

In a very mild area, or where a conservatory is available for winter protection, there are some real show-stoppers to be grown. Phormiums (New Zealand flax) are widely available and are often sold as hardy shrubs. The green forms are relatively tough, but many of the more colourful and most beautiful varieties with red, bronze, pink and purple shades to the foliage are more vulnerable. It is worth giving them winter protection if they have to stay outdoors for the winter (see page 109), but with a little protection in a cold greenhouse or conservatory they should come through in good condition.

Agaves are striking succulents and *A. americana* 'Variegata' is often used as a specimen plant in an urn or other container where a single but striking focal point plant is required. In mild winters mature plants can be left outside, but they will be lost in a cold winter. It is better to preserve your investment by keeping them in a light and frost-free place for the winter. Small ones will look good as houseplants, large specimens will grace any conservatory.

Bananas make impressive foliage plants for the summer, with huge paddle-like evergreen leaves, but these must be housed in a heated greenhouse or conservatory for the winter, and they need a sheltered spot in the summer so that the leaves do not become torn by the wind. Grow large plants like these in a half-barrel on a wheeled board so that you can move them twice a year without too much trouble.

Oranges and lemons

If you have a cool greenhouse or a conservatory in which to overwinter them, and an easy means of moving them once they grow large, oranges and lemons can be kept on a sheltered patio for the summer. *Citrus limon* (lemon) and *Citrus aurantiacum* (Seville orange) can both be stood outdoors for the summer . . . and if the shrubs are mature enough they may even bear fruit.

Bamboos and grasses

Bamboos and many ornamental grasses look good in Oriental-style pots, but choose suitable species. Two of the most desirable bamboos for containers are the tall *Arundinaria murielae* (apple green leaves) and the more compact *Arundinaria viridistriata* (bright green and gold foliage).

A golden grass that has become very popular for containers is *Hakonechloa macra* 'Albo-aurea', a plant with a dreadful name but excellent qualities as a low foliage plant. For something taller and more imposing, pampas grass is an obvious candidate, and it is easy to control in a container. Choose *Cortaderia selloana* 'Pumila', which is a compact form that will reach about 1.2 m (4 ft) in flower.

The appeal of alpines

Stone sinks (genuine or made from 'hypertufa' or reconstituted stone) make a natural-looking home for many choice alpines. There are so many to choose from that individual taste must dictate what is grown, but avoid rampant rock plants like *Alyssum saxatile* and aubrieta: lovely though these are they have no place among the more restrained alpines in a small space. Use a few pieces of rock to help create a miniature 'landscape', and stone chippings to improve the appearance of the surface. One or two very dwarf conifers, such as *Juniperus communis* 'Compressa' will give much-needed height, but choose carefully because many so-called dwarf conifers soon become far too large.

Try a collection of houseleeks (sempervivums) in a sink garden or in a strawberry or herb pot with lots of planting pockets (plant a different kind in each pocket, and several in the top).

Reaching up

In confined areas, such as a balcony or backyard, it makes sense to make the most of all available space. A few trees to give depth and height to the garden and climbers grown up a wall, trellis or wigwam will help to create a sense of balance. If a suitable wall is available, use this by placing large containers close to the wall so that plants can be trained to a trellis. Some climbers, such as ivies and Virginia creeper (*Parthenocissus quinquefolia*) are self-clinging.

With the exception of the annuals, the climbers described in the preceding chapters should of course be considered permanent rather than seasonal inhabitants. Take advantage of the shelter a wall provides to grow slightly tender types, but be wary of climbers with very vigorous, long-reaching root systems, for these will all too soon outgrow the confines of even a large container, and either crack it in half or force themselves out through the drainage holes to root firmly into the surface below – even paving or concrete may not deter some!

Agave americana 'Variegata' makes a truly striking container plant, but except in the very mildest areas it has to be overwintered in a conservatory or frost-free greenhouse.

HANGING BASKETS

Permanently planted hanging baskets are seldom satisfactory. There is very little compost to sustain the plants long-term, and in very cold weather they freeze solid if left outside. An ivy 'ball' sometimes works: the plants will look very sick after severe weather but they usually bounce back again with new spring growth. Place several plants of a small-leaved variety in the top and around the sides, and peg or weave the shoots around the wirework of the basket. In time new growth can be trimmed to produce an attractive ball-like mass of ivy foliage.

Fancy ferns?

Ferns may be the answer for a shady spot where you want to create a lush tranquil atmosphere with plenty of thriving foliage despite poor light.

The shuttlecock or ostrich feather fern (*Matteuccia struthiopteris*) is one of the most eye-catching of all ferns, with tall fronds that grow in a rosette that gives it the appearance of a giant shuttlecock. The royal fern (*Osmunda regalis*) is one of the largest that you are likely to grow – it can reach 1–1.2 m (3–4 ft) but needs a lot of moisture to thrive. Easy and reliable ferns include the lady fern (*Athyrium filix-femina*), male fern (*Dryopteris filix-mas*) and hart's-tongue fern (sold under a variety of names, of which *Asplenium scolopendrium* and *Phyllitis scolopendrium* are two of the common ones).

The royal fern is best grown on its own, but the others will look more interesting if you group them together in a large trough or tub, choosing foliage forms which will contrast effectively with each other. Include some evergreen varieties such as the polystichums, to provide some winter foliage.

Ways with water

A proper pond is preferable to a container pond if there is space for one (the water is easier to 'balance' and keep clear, and it is possible to keep a selection of fish), but on a balcony or in a backyard a mini-pond in a container may be the only way to introduce a water feature. Created in a half-barrel or even a plastic shrub tub, it will give many hours of enjoyment despite its small size.

Planting a pond the size of a shrub tub or half-barrel demands restraint. Choose one small waterlily such as the miniature *Nymphaea pygmaea* 'Helvola' or the slightly larger *N.* 'Froebeli'; add an upright plant like a flowering rush (*Butomus umbellatus*), the miniature reedmace (*Typha minima*) or a variegated rush such as the zebra rush (*Scirpus tabernaemontani* 'Zebrinus'), a double marsh marigold (*Caltha palustris* 'Plena'), and a floater that is easy to control, such as water lettuce (*Pistia stratiotes*). Even this number of plants may be too many . . . if the surface of the water is totally obscured there is not much point in having a mini-pond as a feature.

CHAPTER 6

VEGETABLES, HERBS AND FRUIT

G ROWING EDIBLE CROPS in containers can be fun. They will not feed the family, but it is possible to enjoy a few fresh and tasty fruits and vegetables that you know have not been sprayed with pesticides, and you have the option of choosing varieties for flavour rather than yield or uniformity. Fruit and vegetables do not have to be dull and boring – many crops, from beans and beetroots to lettuces and tomatoes, make attractive ornamental plants for the patio. And where better to have a supply of fresh herbs than in a container close by the kitchen door?

VEGETABLES

Be practical about vegetables. There is little point in wasting a lot of space on crops like potatoes, which you will still have to buy because it is impractical to grow enough to keep even one person supplied. If you want to grow potatoes, choose a very early variety as a treat before the maincrops arrive in the shops. Most of the brassicas, such as cabbages, Brussels sprouts and cauliflowers, need far too much space to be a practical proposition, and few of us find cauliflowers or cabbages appealing to look at. Other crops, such as tomatoes, cut-and-come-again lettuces, and runner beans, on the other hand, can be very attractive if you choose the right varieties and grow them in imaginative ways. And you may be able to grow enough of them to make a real contribution to culinary needs.

The long and short of beans

Runner beans are grown as ornamental climbers in some countries. Try them over an arch or grow them up a wigwam of tall canes (you can buy plastic clips that hold the canes together neatly at the top), or grow them against a wall with a netting support. They are best planted in a large tub. Be prepared to keep the plants well watered and fed.

Choose your colour . . . you can have pretty red and white bicoloured flowers ('Painted Lady'), white ones ('White Achievement'), or pink ('Sunset'), as well as the usual scarlet. Try growing a couple of varieties with different flower colours which can twine around each other.

French beans are usually thought of as compact plants. You can grow these 'normal' types by sowing about ten seeds in a 25–30 cm (10–12 in) pot, but there are climbing versions that are much more decorative. Climbing French beans are not such bold plants as runner beans, but many prefer their culinary qualities. For additional interest, grow a coloured variety such as 'Purple Podded'.

Cucumbers and courgettes

Courgettes and cucumbers are practical propositions for a patio tub, but choose the variety with care. Outdoor ridge cucumbers are not to everyone's taste, but 'Bush Champion' is ideal for patio containers, and it fruits prolifically. Some greenhouse varieties can be grown outdoors too, but they need a warm, sheltered position, and you must provide a cane for support. Choose one of the all-female F1 hybrid varieties. Much depends on the summer, but it is possible to grow cucumbers on your patio that rival for taste anything you could buy in a supermarket.

Courgettes are easier but they are large plants and you can fit only one to a fairly large tub. Where you need something decorative, choose a yellow variety such as 'Gold Rush'.

Beetroots and carrots

Beetroots and carrots can be grown on their own, in growing bags or even in windowboxes, but they do not make an especially attractive feature. Both have pretty foliage, however, which we often overlook. Beetroot is occasionally grown as a foliage summer bedding plant, where its reddish-purple leaves contrast well with silver-leaved plants and yellow flowers. The same principle can be used in containers, and carrots too can be used where some feathery foliage would act as a foil for all the bright flowers. Once the vegetables are large enough, simply pull them out and leave the other plants to continue the display alone.

For a few tasty roots to supplement those you buy, grow these as foliage plants among colourful bedding for a bit of fun, but start them off in small pots or plugs of compost, as they will not compete with the bedding plants if simply sown between them. The most practical way to grow beetroots and carrots is in old growing bags.

Whichever method you use, choose small round or stump-rooted carrots such as 'Early French Frame', and beetroots that produce just one seedling per seed cluster, such as 'Monopoly'.

Rhubarb chard and leaf beet

These vegetables are not to everyone's taste, but they are pretty enough to grow purely as ornamentals. Rhubarb chard has long bright crimson stalks and dark green crinkled leaves. Silver or seakale beet, also known as Swiss chard, is similar in size and stature with bright green leaf blades and white leaf stalks. Either will

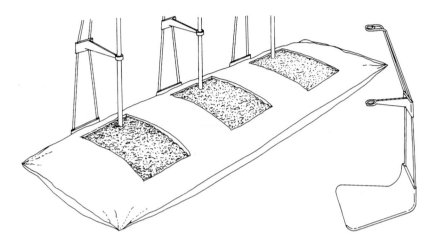

Fig 6 *Growing bags have insufficient depth of compost to support canes for tall plants such as tomatoes. Use proprietary growing bag cane supports to overcome this problem.*

make an attractive foliage plant, but try planting the two together for an even bolder display.

The place for these quite large plants is as a centrepiece in a large tub, perhaps a half-barrel, with summer bedding plants around the edge. If you like these vegetables a lot, then grow them alone (or the two together) in a trough. That way you will have more leaves to harvest and they need no other companions to create the kind of bold display that seldom fails to attract attention.

Lettuces and tomatoes

Tomatoes and lettuces are the mainstay of summer salads, and both can be grown successfully in containers.

Grow tomatoes in growing bags if you want a heavy crop and a wide choice of varieties but are not too bothered about appearances. There are excellent bush varieties like 'Red Alert' and 'Tornado' that require minimal staking and do not require the constant removal of sideshoots. Normal upright kinds require supports, which can be bought from garden centres (Fig. 6).

If you want your tomatoes to be more decorative, choose a variety that you can grow in a windowbox or hanging basket. These generally have small cherry-type fruits, but they are produced in abundance in large clusters. 'Tumbler' has a cascading habit that makes it suitable for a hanging basket or the edge of a windowbox. If you want an attractive tomato to grow in a pot or tub on the patio try 'Totem'. The growth is clustered around a thick central stem that is largely self-supporting. Although it will grow taller in a growing bag or if

Opposite: *Barrels make a good home for a collection of herbs if you drill planting holes in the sides. A barrel of this size will accommodate a wide range of culinary herbs.*

planted in the ground, in a pot it often remains as compact as 45 cm (18 in), yet can produce 1.4–2.7 kg (3–6 lb) of medium sized tomatoes.

Lettuces should be chosen and grown with thought. Varieties that form a heart can be grown very successfully in growing bags, and this is an ideal crop for old bags that were perhaps used for tomatoes last year. Hearting lettuces are not a practical proposition, however, for a decorative windowbox, where a glaring gap is left every time one is harvested.

Choose a non-hearting cut-and-come-again type for windowboxes and other containers. If you take a few leaves from different plants, they will remain attractive for a long period, and the oak-leaf shaped leaves are pretty on their own or planted in front of flowers. Grow the bright green 'Salad Bowl' and 'Red Salad Bowl', alternating the plants for a really pretty as well as practical crop of lettuces. If you want to try a third variety 'Carnival' adds yet another colour . . . the dark green leaves are tinged red but lack the visual punch of the other two.

Bagged potatoes

An old growing bag will make a practical home for a few early potatoes. This is not a practical way to grow maincrop potatoes, but a few early new potatoes is a treat worth having.

Choose an early variety and space out about four tubers in the growing bag, making sure they are covered. Do this in early spring unless you live in a very cold district. The shoots must be protected from frost, so be prepared to cover the plants with newspapers or other protection if frost is forecast. Better still, place the growing bag on a board that can be lifted, with a helper, and moved indoors or into a greenhouse whenever it is too cold.

Harvest the potatoes while they are young – the compost and foliage should have protected the tubers enough to make any kind of earthing up or blanching unnecessary.

ORNAMENTAL KALES AND CABBAGES

Ornamental cabbages, with pink, red, purple, or white leaves that look almost like a giant flower, are not new, but together with the ornamental kales (which have more divided leaves) they have become fashionable. They are now often sold in garden centres and even by supermarkets and florists, but they are very easy to grow from seed yourself . . . and much cheaper. You do not even need a greenhouse.

You would not normally grow ornamental cabbages and kales to eat, but they are edible and if you really want to grow cabbages among the flowers this is one way. Do not expect a good heart in your cabbages, however, as they do not colour well until the night temperature drops to about 10°C (50°F), and towards the late autumn the centre begins to open.

HERBS

Some herbs make excellent container plants – bay is a classic. Others, such as mint, are better in a container because it prevents them making a take-over bid into the territory of surrounding plants. The majority, such as thymes, marjorams and chives, tolerate a contained life provided the light is good. Most herbs prefer a hot, sunny position.

Herb pots with planting pockets in the sides look attractive, but beware of those with an inward-sloping neck if you plan to plant a shrub like bay or sage in the top. When the shrub grows too large and needs repotting, it will be very difficult to remove the root-ball without breaking the pot or severely damaging the root system. Choose a pot with straight sides or restrict the planting in the top to small perennials or annuals.

Specimen plants

Avoid planting your bay in a box of mixed herbs. Small specimens have too few leaves to risk harvesting for the pot, and more mature specimens will be too large for a windowbox or trough. Grow your bay in a tub or half-barrel and clip it to an attractive pyramid. To create an impression of elegance, try growing a pair either side of the front or kitchen door in white-painted Versailles tubs. Bays can be bought trained into more elaborate shapes, but these are not so practical if you want to keep clipping a few leaves for the kitchen.

Most elegant of all are bays with a clear stem trained into a kind of corkscrew shape. These are particularly effective viewed against a light-coloured wall.

Rosemary cannot be clipped to such a neat formal shape as bay, but let it grace your patio with its small but pretty blue flowers set against pleasant grey-green evergreen foliage. The flowers can appear mid winter and continue well into early summer, and even beyond.

The sage usually used for cooking has plain green leaves, but there are variegated forms that make attractive container plants and can still be used for flavouring. Try three different kinds in the one shrub tub: *Salvia officinalis* 'Icterina' (green and gold), 'Purpurascens' (stems and foliage suffused purple), and 'Tricolor' (grey-green and creamy white, suffused purple and pink).

Growing bag collections

The best place for a mint is in a growing bag, from which it will find it difficult to escape. Mint does not have to be boring as there are many variegated kinds, including the green and gold ginger mint and white-splashed variegated apple mint, but do not grow these to the exclusion of the popular spearmint (used for mint sauce). You should be able to grow a collection of at least four mints in a growing bag.

Sorrels are also at home in an old growing bag.

Windowboxes and troughs

Windowboxes and troughs offer scope for some really creative planting, with lots of thymes, marjorams, chives, and perhaps a few less pretty but nevertheless

This glass-fibre trough contains a surprisingly good collection of herbs for its size: rue, Thymus serpyllum 'Pink Chintz', variegated apple mint, ginger mint and hyssop at the front, with chives, marjoram, pineapple sage and Welsh onion at the back.

KEEP A SENSE OF PROPORTION

Herb windowboxes created for an occasion, such as a flower show, often contain plants that are impractical or unsuitable in a windowbox that has to remain looking good all summer, and possibly beyond. There is no place in a practical herb window-box or trough for giants like fennel, or vigorous bushy plants like lemon balm. Very young bay trees are sometimes included, but these can only be for temporary effect: if you want bay leaves for the kitchen grow a bush in a tub.

useful herbs such as tarragon. Some people add plants like nasturtiums (the seeds are sometimes pickled) and pot marigold (calendulas), grown for their bright edible petals. Mixing these with the more basic herbs calls for great skill otherwise they will dominate the collection. For more variety grow a few variegated mints (keep them in their pots to control their growth).

The ordinary culinary thyme (*Thymus vulgaris*) has pretty flowers but the

Courgettes make interesting patio plants, and 'Gold Rush', which is yellow, is particularly attractive.

foliage is unexciting. Add one or two coloured or variegated kinds, such as *T.v.* 'Aureus' (a lovely bright yellow) or the variegated lemon-scented thyme *T.* × *citriodorus* 'Silver Queen'.

Adding flavour to the flowers

Use fennel, which produces feathery green or bronze foliage on shoots that often reach 1.8 m (6 ft), as a centrepiece in a large tub or a half-barrel. Plant summer bedding around the base, perhaps ornamental tobacco plants (*Nicotiana*) or use the red foliage of beetroot or rhubarb chard around the green form of fennel.

Use parsley to produce cushions of green foliage amid bright summer bedding plants, in windowboxes and troughs, or plant chives as a flower in a mixed arrangement: its small heads of pink flowers resemble thrift from a distance, and you can just clip off a few of the grass-like leaves for the kitchen with a pair of scissors when you need them.

Parsley balls

Make a ball of parsley by planting up a wire basket with seedlings. To produce the ball-shaped effect make sure the basket is well planted in the sides as well as the top, and keep the basket in good light, turning it at least every second day. Be sure to harvest just a few shoots at once, and remove them from various parts of the 'ball'.

WHEEL BARRELS

Make a feature of an unusual container, such as an old wheelbarrow or a barrel with holes drilled in the side to provide planting pockets. These hold more compost than most windowboxes and pots, so most herbs should do well in them. Unfortunately there is always a shady side to a barrel, and on that side some plants may perform poorly. If the wheelbarrow still has a working wheel, you can move it around . . . not only to catch the sun if necessary but also to bring it to a position of prominence for those few weeks when everything in it looks good. Containers with herbaceous herbs are uninspiring for much of the year.

FRUIT

A mini-orchard with dwarf fruit trees in pots can become reality, and you will not have to wait years to pick your first apples if you choose suitable trees and rootstocks. Wall-trained peaches, cherries, and even plums are all possible, but unless you plan to make fruit the main feature of your container garden, settle for apples and strawberries, which are really reliable in pots.

Apples

If there are other apple trees in your neighbourhood, you can grow just one apple tree if space is limited. If you are not aware of other trees that could act as pollinators plant at least two that flower at the same time (the nursery or garden centre should be able to advise) to ensure a good crop.

Buy trees grafted on to a dwarfing rootstock such as M9 or M26 (M27 is acceptable), and grow in 30–38 cm (12–15 in) pots. Train them as dwarf pyramids.

Flagpole or Ballerina apple trees have become popular for small gardens, as these very narrow trees crop early and take up very little space. There are several varieties from which to choose. They can look rather stark in pots, however, and you may prefer to choose a conventional variety that you like for flavour and grow it as a dwarf pyramid that has more 'presence' than a narrow, upright tree.

Pears, plums and peaches

These are less reliable croppers in pots, but if you fancy pears choose a couple on Quince A or Quince C rootstocks (you will need two for cross-pollination). Train them as dwarf pyramids.

Most plums also need a pollinator, but 'Denniston's Superb' is self-fertile. Buy a plant grafted into 'Pixy' rootstock and train it by the festooning method (Fig. 7).

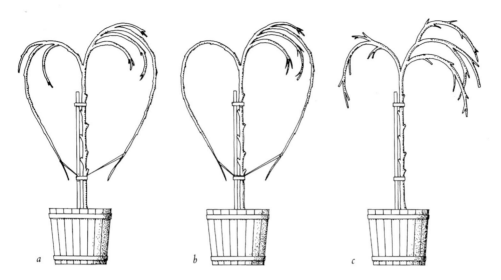

Fig 7 *Train plums into festoons to keep them compact enough for a container. Prune back the sideshoots in late summer, then bend over the main stem, tying it in place (**a**). New shoots will develop towards the top of the tree, and these should be tied down in a similar way (**b**). The following spring release the ties (the branches should have 'set' into a festoon shape) (**c**), and cut out the main shoot to prevent further upward growth.*

Strawberry time

Traditional strawberry tubs are terracotta with planting holes in the sides and spaces for several plants in the top. There are many modern plastic versions and some have more holes than a normal terracotta pot, but you may not find them so acceptable visually. Some plastic types do not contain drainage holes, and these may become waterlogged in wet weather, though they are fine for a greenhouse.

Replace the strawberry plants every second year to maintain vigorous, healthy stock. Grow summer-fruiting varieties if you want a short cropping period between late spring and late summer (time will depend on variety), or perpetual or autumn-fruiting kinds if you want the heaviest crop in early autumn (they produce some earlier fruit). Try two or three plants of several different varieties if you want to spread the cropping over a long period, but be prepared for relatively few strawberries at any one time.

Tower pots and strawberry pots are expensive to buy and should be filled with a good compost; if you also buy new plants every couple of years your strawberries can become expensive. Propagating your own plants from runners will help save money, but the plant quality will deteriorate over the years. Bags may be best if you want to keep the cost down. Old growing bags can be used for a strawberry crop before you throw them away. This eliminates the cost of the container and compost ... and the plants are often easier to look after in a growing bag.

CHAPTER 7

CREATIVE WITH CONTAINERS

THERE IS MORE to creative container gardening than simply cultivating the most floriferous and wonderfully colourful pots and baskets. The containers themselves have a role to play, and how they are grouped or arranged, or perhaps placed in splendid isolation as a focal point, help to determine the overall impression. Choice containers add a touch of style and elegance, but they are not essential: some of the most eye-catching displays are created from containers like old Wellington boots, shoes, empty plastic fruit juice containers and similar discarded items. All of these have the potential to look grotesque, but suitably grouped and positioned as a clear expression of fun or exuberance they become beautiful examples of container gardening at its best.

A container right for one place may be wrong for another. What is appropriate flanking a formal front door may lack the sense of extravagance required for a balcony garden that has to reflect the need for colour and foliage cover. An interesting container with a bold foliage plant may be lost against a background of other plants but look stunning viewed against the background of a white or pink painted wall. Plastic containers that appeal to one person may be abhorrent to another. There are no absolutes, and the best containers and plant combinations are those that are right for the individual. That is why the planting combinations and container ideas in this book and others should be a starting point for creative container gardening, and not some final goal. Use other people's ideas as a starting point, and adapt them to suit your own taste. The best examples of container gardening combine inspiration and good cultivation.

APPROPRIATE CONTAINERS

The practicalities of various materials are outlined on pages 100–1, but your choice should also be an aesthetic one.

Opposite: *Containers can be placed in flower beds and borders, where they will often create a localized focal point. Here the soft colours of a fuchsia and pale variegated ivy create a subtle and tasteful effect.*

Fig 8 *Try to match container to surroundings. A classic style like this will look good in a large country garden but may be inappropriate for a small suburban front garden on an estate.*

Inexpensive plastic containers are adequate if what goes in them is a fountain of flowers, many of which cascade over the edge, hiding most of the container anyway. An expensive terracotta trough with intricate moulding would probably be wasted. Similarly, on a balcony garden or a patio where modern materials predominate, a stone urn in classical style can look out of place and character (Fig. 8).

Plastic is also appropriate in the form of windowboxes used as 'liners' to drop into a more decorative outer container (Fig. 9), perhaps made from wood and painted to match the house. As mentioned earlier, to get the best from containers the year round it makes sense to have spare ones planted up with later flowerers to replace those which have finished their display. This is a more appealing idea if the containers are relatively inexpensive and light.

Weight is important on balconies and roof gardens, and plastic and glass-fibre are sensible materials for these situations. This does not mean abandoning elegance: glass-fibre is used to recreate very convincing replicas of materials like lead . . . but of course at a mere fraction of the weight.

Large plastic pots sound unappealing, but those over about 30 cm (12 in) wide are likely to be made of a much tougher material than ordinary plant pots, and the colour matches terracotta more closely. Grow large, totally hardy shrubs and small trees that can be left in position for years, in terracotta pots or tubs (they look better and benefit from the additional weight that helps stability), but if you want to grow a large plant such as a datura, that has to be moved indoors or into a greenhouse for the winter, a large plastic pot will make the job of transferring it in and out very much easier.

If plastic containers are to be on show, then colour and finish must be taken into consideration. Because plastic is easily moulded some are produced with a wooden finish, but no matter how good the moulding the colour is far from convincing. Manufacturers produce plastic containers in many colours: white and green are popular, but white can be too glaring and green never looks as harmonious as one might imagine. One of the best colours is dark brown, which does not intrude in the same way as lighter colours.

For containers which are to perform a decorative as well as practical function, it is usually worth investing in something attractive and durable which will suit its surroundings. Terracotta and reconstituted stone nearly always enhance the plants without being obtrusive, and are available in modern and traditional shapes, both plain or highly ornate. Concrete tubs and bowls usually come in strong, simple outlines which look best in a modern setting, while wood is another material which seems to lend itself to any style, whether in the form of a weathered half-barrel in a farmhouse courtyard or a pair of painted Versailles tubs setting off the front of a Georgian town house.

Fig 9 (*a*) *Large troughs and windowboxes like this one made from glass-reinforced cement are too expensive and heavy to have a number of them to use in rotation as plants pass their best. Instead, use several liner boxes that will fit the outer box and grow a succession of plants in these, replacing them as necessary.* (*b*) *Inexpensive plastic containers can be improved with a false front, like this one made from a piece of wood with the bark left on (try a florist for a piece of cork that may be suitable).*

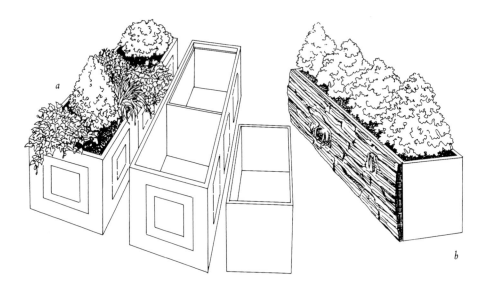

Fig 10 *Grouping containers can be more effective than dotting them around the garden individually. The grouping itself can be quite artistic, and if the plants in one container are not at their best this will hardly be noticed if the others are attractive.*

KEEP A SENSE OF PROPORTION

A low, ornately decorated trough or shallow, terracotta windowbox needs a few choice alpines or compact summer bedding plants such as fibrous-rooted begonias or perhaps pansies. A tall urn or vase calls for pendulous plants to tumble down the sides.

POSITIONING FOR EFFECT

A particularly striking container or plant may require isolation so that it becomes a focal point, but most are better grouped together rather than dotted around the garden or patio (Fig. 10). Tall pots often look more effective with a few lower, flatter containers placed in front. Use containers and plants of different heights to create a curtain effect: taller shrubs or small trees at the back, medium-sized bright and bushy plants in front to create interest towards the base of the back-row plants, and small low troughs with alpines or dwarf bedding plants in front to mask the base and some of the containers in the middle row. Avoid regimented rows, however, and stagger them to create an informal assembly that looks as though the plants could be growing together in a natural setting.

Opposite: Unusual containers add a sense of fun and old wheelbarrows are a popular choice. They need to be packed with bushy bedding plants so that they appear to brim over the barrow.

Making an entrance

An entrance, by its very nature, is important. It creates an impression – negative or positive – that tells visitors something about you and your home (Fig. 11). Avoid being pretentious, however, and don't have Grecian urns by the front door of a small terraced house or Versailles tubs planted with elegant dwarf palms at the entrance to the drive of a modern estate house.

If you have a formal entrance and a rather grand front door, then let this be reflected by a similarly formal arrangement of containers and a restrained planting. For a town terrace with a tiny front garden, a tall bamboo in a very decorative pot, or bright spring and summer bedding belching from the top of a couple of chimney pots, may be more suitable. Old chimney pots are very appropriate containers for a city garden, especially in older areas where chimneys are common, but it might be better to have a group of, say, three in different sizes to one side of the door, rather than a single pot each side.

A house on a modern housing estate may be enhanced by modern materials and containers in abstract or unconventional shapes. Again, a group to one side of the door may look better than a formal flanking pair.

Porches provide an ideal opportunity for container gardening – they can look like mini greenhouses in summer, and even in winter should look good if used to house those plants that benefit from a little winter protection, such as phormiums.

Fig 11 *A plain door can be transformed into a welcoming vista for approaching visitors. Group several containers together, with plants at various heights, for strong impact (**a**), or adopt a formal approach with a pair of formally clipped plants such as bay or box (**b**).*

Some porches can be quite gloomy but there are always shade-loving foliage plants that can be used to create a good impression. If you have a tall indoor yucca in the house, try it out in the porch for the summer, and group other foliage pot plants such as dracaenas around it. Be adventurous: pot up a clump of rhubarb from the garden and use this as a striking foliage plant along with more tender kinds. Paint a picture with foliage – it can be abstract – and make sure you introduce something a little unusual to provide a talking point for visitors.

Stepping up the interest

Steps concentrate the eye, and the longer the flight of steps the more dominant and harsh they appear. But they provide an excellent focus for containers used in a variety of ways (Fig. 12). Use pots of plants at the base or top, and if there are pillars on which you can stand shallow containers use these to grow cascading plants to shower and soften the outline. If the treads are deep and wide enough, use free-standing pots stepped up the whole flight. Unless the steps are exceptionally wide, keep the free-standing pots to one side of the flight for reasons of safety.

Where steps lead down to a basement area or backyard, use one or two climbers to clothe the house wall. A Virginia creeper (*Parthenocissus quinquefolia*) planted in a large tub near the base of the steps will provide quick cover, but only for the summer; an ivy will make an evergreen curtain but grows more slowly.

Fig 12 *Basement gardens with dominant steps and overpowering walls can be improved by growing climbers up the walls and using troughs or windowboxes with trailers fixed to the railings. For added impact place a few pots of bright or bold plants on the steps, if they are wide enough (otherwise place them at the top or bottom of the flight for safety).*

Above: *This conifer shows how effective a container plant can be as a focal point. The attractive container and distinctive paving all emphasize its role in attracting the eye.*

Ways with walls

Walls provide a useful backdrop for plants, and often shelter, too. In a moderately large garden they provide an ideal home for many kinds of climbers, but in a backyard or courtyard garden, or even on a balcony, walls can seem overpowering and even gloomy. Turn them to your advantage, however, by making a feature of them.

Railings are often used for safety where steps go down to basements, and sometimes where steps are needed for high level access to the home. Grow clematis and other climbers up these, but avoid anything too rampant – it must be easy to keep the handrail clear. It may be possible to fix boxes to the railings and use trailers such as small-leaved ivies, and in summer creeping Jenny (*Lysimachia nummularia*) and canary creeper (*Tropaeolum canariense*). Both will cascade downwards, and the canary creeper will also climb up and along the railings.

Opposite: *Wide steps can be improved with plenty of containers. The dominant plants in these are the daisy-like mesembryanthemums, which need a sunny position to make this kind of stunning display.*

Transform backyard, basement and courtyard walls into a source of light and cheerfulness by painting them white or some other pale colour. Then paint most of your woodwork in a matching pale colour – including trellises fixed to the wall. Plant climbers in tubs to provide a refreshing coat of verdant foliage for the summer: it does not matter if they are deciduous because the exposed light wall will help to reflect more much-needed light in winter.

Use plenty of wall baskets, or for a bit of character an old manger fixed to the wall to provide seasonal colour. Reproduction mangers are available if you are unable to find the genuine thing, and these are useful because they hold more compost than most wall baskets. Paint the metalwork black to provide a striking contrast to white-painted walls.

Against this transformation from dull brick to a light and cheerful backdrop for plants, paint your picture in plants. You may prefer hot, vibrant colours such as bright red geraniums (pelargoniums), scarlet salvias and brash nasturtiums, or instead choose to have a scheme that looks cool and co-ordinated. If you have chosen white walls, some of them covered with the fresh green foliage of climbers, an all-white theme may appeal. Tubs of white petunias, pots of white marguerites, white busy Lizzies, and perhaps white alyssum growing in cracks in the paving. You need a focal point in this kind of garden, perhaps an attractive white bust or figure on a plinth in one corner.

Avoid rows of half-baskets or wall-mounted windowboxes all at the same height. Fix them at different heights so that the eye does not travel along them in a straight line. Have more than one row to make the most of an otherwise blank and wasted wall, but stagger them so that they overlap and are spaced well apart vertically and horizontally (Fig. 13).

Fig 13 *Courtyard and basement gardens need plenty of plants to brighten the walls. Windowboxes are an ideal solution, but stagger them so that they do not form rigid vertical rows. A pyramid like this makes a bold feature.*

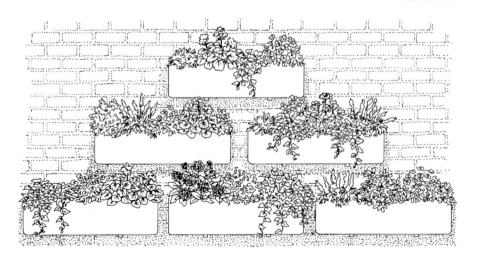

Windowsills and balconies

Use plenty of evergreen trailers to hang from balconies or windowboxes. Ivies and some cotoneasters, such as *C. salicifolius* 'Gnom', will trail down outside quite a way. Other people get most of the benefit from the green curtain that is created, but it is tremendously satisfying to know that your balcony looks good from the outside as well as from the home side.

If the balcony has a solid edge, hang windowboxes on the inside (not on the top where they are a potential danger, unless very firmly fixed), with the 'outside' trailers hanging over the outside edge. Trailers on the inside edge can cascade down to provide a second curtain of cascaders. If the balcony has railings instead of a wall, keep the containers at floor level where they are more stable and allow the trailers to hang through the railings. Climbers can be allowed to grow up and through the railings – but bear in mind that this will cast shade and your flowers may not bloom so well.

Use lots of exotic indoor pot plants on a balcony during the summer once you have established shelter from damaging winds.

Make the most of balcony walls by fixing wall baskets and windowboxes to these, above the level of most of the plants in floor-standing containers.

SOMETHING DIFFERENT

A sense of fun never comes amiss except in the most formal type of garden, but avoid being too outrageous with the choice of containers.

Wheelbarrows look appropriate whether the garden is traditional style or strictly modern. A really old-fashioned wooden barrow looks great painted in bright colours such as apple green and a cheery red, but an old modern metal one is perfectly acceptable once filled with summer bedding that includes plenty of cascaders.

Paint some old paint tins white, then add 'drips' of an appropriate colour – try red drips for red flowers. Press old car tyres into use: there are many ways of 'converting' them into containers but a simple method is to paint them white outside and stack two or three on top of one another. Plant trailers such as ivies as a permanent feature to cascade down the sides, and use seasonal plants in the top.

Plastic barrels can be cut down, drainage holes made, then painted to provide a home for shrubs such as hydrangeas. You do not have to be particularly artistic – choose a simple design or copy the designs traditionally used for canal boats.

Old chimney pots make distinctive containers, ideal for a mixture of upright and trailing plants. Group the pots together in a small collection so the variety of pot designs is also a feature.

Containers of all kinds – buckets, kettles, clogs and gardening boots, even washing-up bowls can be used – but the key is to use them in context. A bright red plastic washing-up bowl could look dreadful by the front door or on a formal patio, but brimful of beautiful flowers in juxtaposition with the clothes line or drier it suddenly has a sense of purpose and becomes part of a design.

Use your imagination and be creative, but never lose sight of taste and design.

CHAPTER 8

KNOW-HOW

NEWCOMERS TO CONTAINER gardening often assume that the key to success lies with the choice of plants, or the effect of some special grouping that looks particularly good. In reality what brings success or leads to dismal disappointment are practical things, like compost, feeding and watering. Some of the most magnificent displays I have seen have used everyday plants like petunias, fuchsias, pansies and geraniums. A display of petunias in large baskets that cascade down to meet more petunias erupting from a collection of containers of different heights can produce a sheet of colour perhaps 2.4 m (8 ft) high with hardly a trace of a container visible if the plants are really well grown. The most elaborately planted baskets and windowboxes can look pathetically undistinguished if the plants are not looked after. It is the health of the plants, and not the amount of money that you spend on containers or the number of plants that you buy, that will ultimately determine success or otherwise.

In no other aspect of gardening (except perhaps for greenhouse and house plants) is care and know-how so vital. You can forget to feed your shrubs in the garden and nothing drastic will happen; you may never water your bedding plants in beds and borders once they are established and they will almost certainly continue to bloom prolifically. If you neglect watering containers for just one day in the hottest weeks of summer, sensitive plants such as lobelia will bring their efforts to an abrupt end. Feeding is not the marginal benefit that it might be for plants in beds and borders – container gardening is a form of intensive cultivation where plants compete with each other as effectively as weeds compete for light and nutrients in beds and borders.

CHOOSING CONTAINERS

Containers are often chosen purely for appearance, but there are practical considerations too.

Size and shape

Choose containers that hold plenty of compost. Shallow ones will dry out more quickly and with less compost the plants require feeding and watering more frequently. Balance this consideration with the weight to be lifted or supported, especially with windowboxes and hanging baskets. With windowboxes the depth of the compost is important from a maintenance viewpoint, but the width from back to front will dictate whether you can fit one, two, three or even more rows of plants in, and this affects the type of display that can be created. Length is the least important dimension. If the ledge is long, use two smaller boxes, which will be much easier to lift than a long one. Once plants bush out the join will hardly be noticed; alternatively fix a false front that spans the two boxes and makes them look like one.

The minimum practical depth for a windowbox or trough is 20 cm (8 in), as about 2.5 cm (1 in) will be taken up with a drainage layer and as much again must be left above compost level to make watering easy. Only a few plants, such as alpines, will be happy in shallower windowboxes and troughs.

Hanging baskets should be as large as possible, but even with a lightweight compost the support may be the limiting factor. A 30 cm (12 in) basket is a good compromise between display and weight. If a very strong support is available, a larger basket will look even better.

Tubs, pots and urns almost always hold a more adequate amount of compost for the surface area available for planting. But watch out for containers with a narrow neck if you are likely to plant with perennials that have to be moved to a larger container after a few years: you will have to damage the plant or the pot in extracting the plant.

HOW MANY TO A CONTAINER?

The number of plants you can cram into a container obviously depends on the size of both container and plants, but beyond that you should consider the effect desired. An elegant bamboo in a Japanese style glazed container would be spoilt by adding bedding plants or bulbs around the base; a plant with a bold profile, such as a datura or *Fatsia japonica* needs to stand in isolation to impose its full stature on the scene. On the other hand spring-flowering bulbs should be packed as close together as possible for real impact, to create the impression of established clumps. (In borders in the garden the bulbs are probably touching as they have multiplied over the years.) Even with close planting the effect can look sparse in early spring, so bushy biennials such as forget-me-nots can also be packed in to provide more cover.

Beware of introducing too many *types* of plants, however, otherwise the arrangement will look excessively 'busy' and fussy. Some gardeners like to cram in many different kinds of plants in one container, but often a planting scheme with just two or three different kinds looks more 'designed', and single-subject plantings can be very striking.

Material considerations

Most shapes of container are available in a wide range of materials (Fig. 14).

Fig 14 *There are materials and styles to suit all tastes and pockets. These are (**a**) terracotta with acanthus design, (**b**) plastic with roman design, (**c**) plain plastic (avoid garish colours), (**d**) a metal reproduction manger, (**e**) wooden, (**f**) glass-reinforced plastic (glass-fibre) in an eighteenth-century style.*

Plastic containers are cheap and widely available. Some of the cheapest and most brash look glaringly unattractive and will probably be short-lived (they become brittle after a season or two and crack or split). The more expensive types are usually of better quality, and polypropylene shrub tubs and large pots are robust and generally more pleasing visually.

Glass-reinforced cement looks a bit like reconstituted stone, but can be cast in thinner sections. Containers made from this are generally capacious and elegant, but expensive and not widely available. They are very long lasting.

Glass-reinforced plastic (glass-fibre) is used to make some very attractive and elegant containers, including windowboxes that look like lead. They are generally large enough to hold plenty of compost, and should last for many years.

Reconstituted stone is used for large, elegant containers in classic styles. It brings the traditional style of container down to a reasonable cost. Most designs hold enough compost even for demanding plants, but weight makes them unsuitable for plants that have to be moved around (for winter protection, for instance).

Concrete lacks the finely detailed moulding that can be achieved with reconstituted stone, and needs more weathering to look good, but it is cheaper and the weight makes it a good choice for small trees and large shrubs.

Recycled cellulose fibre lacks visual appeal (peat brown with the texture of thick papier mâché), and is unlikely to last more than one or two seasons outdoors; on a protected balcony it may last a little longer. Despite these draw-backs such containers are cheap enough to be useful for seasonal summer bedding plants, and once established with some cascading plants as masking, look perfectly acceptable. Use a lot of them together rather than dot them around, so that the containers tend to hide each other (except the front ones, which you can plant with trailers), then the overall impression will be of a mass of flowers.

Timber can be expensive, and unless very well preserved will rot after a few years. Its great advantage is that it is easy to paint if you want to produce a co-ordinated colour scheme with the paintwork of the house, or simply to provide some gay and even outrageously bright containers. You can paint pretty designs on them with acrylic paints to make them unique to you.

Terracotta has a timeless appeal and a natural warmth that allows it to blend in with almost any garden setting and style. Troughs and windowboxes are available as well as a whole range of pots and tubs in many shapes and sizes, plain or ornate. Most plants seem to like terracotta too, although there are exceptions, due to its porosity, such as daturas, hostas and other moisture lovers.

IS IT FROSTPROOF?

Some terracotta containers imported from warmer climates are not reliably frost-proof. In winter they may crumble or split as the moisture absorbed by the terra-cotta freezes and expands. It is not easy to tell simply by looking at the pot, so ask the seller for an assurance that it is frostproof.

Pots that curve inwards at the top may still be damaged if you leave them full of compost, even if technically frostproof: as the frozen compost expands the pot may not be able to accommodate the pressure and could crack.

Cleaning and decorating

Old wooden barrels will probably not have contained anything more harmful than beer, and by the time you obtain them it is unlikely that they will require any cleaning. Old paint tins are not likely to cause any problems either: provided the paint is thoroughly dry (pour out any surplus and then leave the tin to dry), you can plant without further preparation.

Wash out containers that might have contained dangerous or unknown chemicals, such as plastic barrels and tubs used as bulk packing. Use washing-up liquid to help remove traces of the chemicals, then flush out with plenty of fresh water.

If you wish to retain the natural appearance of a wooden windowbox or tub, apply several coats of an exterior grade polyurethane varnish. Coloured timber preservatives can be quite acceptable visually and will help to preserve the wood better than a varnish.

Use an exterior grade gloss paint over a primer and undercoat if you wish to paint tubs and windowboxes a bright colour, perhaps to match the house paint-work. The same paint used for the exterior woodwork of the house will be suitable.

Use acrylic paints (which you can buy from an art shop) if you want to be artistic and paint a floral or other design on a wooden windowbox or a cut-down plastic barrel.

Paint pots (whether metal or plastic) can be painted with an exterior emulsion or gloss paint to cover the background printing. Then use a gloss paint if you want to add further decoration.

Drainage

All containers, except those used for aquatic plants, must have drainage holes. If you are improvising with old containers that lack suitable drainage holes, remember to make some before you plant.

Prepare barrels and other wooden containers by boring out half a dozen 12–25 mm ($\frac{1}{2}$–1 in) holes with a brace and bit.

Plastic containers sometimes split when you try to drill out holes, so try placing adhesive tape on either side before drilling, or heat the end of a metal rod to melt holes in the plastic.

The number and size of holes are less important than the assurance that they are not blocked. Always place a layer of good free-draining material such as gravel or broken pots in the bottom before adding compost, and raise the container slightly on bricks or small blocks so that water can drain away (this will also help to prevent wood rotting). Small 'feet' can be bought for some terracotta troughs and windowboxes, and these can also be used for other types of container too.

CONCERNING COMPOST

A visit to any garden centre will reveal a bewildering range of composts. Not only brands but types. Apart from the traditional loam-based and peat-based composts there are peat-substitute composts based on coconut fibre and other materials, various kinds of specialist container composts for hanging baskets, and tubs, or for specific types of plants. Add to that the considerable brand variations and the problem of choosing the best is obvious. Yet choice of compost is one of the most important decisions in container gardening.

There is no one ideal compost for all containers, so split the decision into uses.

Permanently planted tubs and troughs Use a loam-based compost. It has better reserves of nutrients and the weight will add stability for trees and shrubs.

Seasonal plants in tubs and troughs Use either loam-based or peat or peat-substitute compost – whichever you have available.

Permanently planted windowboxes Use a loam-based compost if weight is not a problem. Where weight has to be kept down, a container compost (but not one based on loam alone), which has added nutrients, is a good compromise.

Seasonally planted windowboxes Where weight is an important consideration, use a peat-based or peat-substitute compost.

Hanging baskets Use a special hanging basket compost or a peat or peat-substitute compost.

Composts have the pH adjusted to suit the majority of plants, and even peat-based composts are not necessarily acid. If you want to grow a plant that needs an acid soil, choose an ericaceous compost. Both loam-based and peat-based ericaceous composts are readily available at garden centres. With this kind of

Glass-reinforced concrete can be cast in much thinner sections than ordinary concrete, making windowboxes and troughs like this a practical proposition. Although heavy, they are long-lasting and generally have generous dimensions that make them suitable for dwarf shrubs.

compost it is possible to grow acid-loving plants like rhododendrons even if the garden soil is very alkaline.

Organic gardeners will prefer to use an 'organic' compost, such as one based on cow manure and peat or composted bark and animal manures. They are likely to be more expensive than conventional composts but should grow good plants. They will still require feeding during the growing season.

BEWARE OF BRAND VARIATIONS

John Innes compost is made to a standard formula in bags carrying the JI manufacturers' seal and results should vary little. Use JI potting compost No. 3 for permanent plantings, No. 2 for seasonal plants. Peat-based and peat-substitute composts vary considerably from one brand to another. Try buying two or three brands then use them for identical containers (windowboxes, baskets) with similar plants: if one outperforms the others keep to that one in future years.

Peat substitutes

Many gardeners like to play their part in conservation by keeping the use of peat to a minimum. Among the alternatives now available are those based on chipped and treated bark and coconut fibre. It is probably unwise to use any of these for permanent plantings, but they are worth trying for a seasonal container. Results can be very good or very poor, so before changing over to one particular brand, ask other gardeners about their experiences, and try out several alongside traditional composts, and judge for yourself which are worth buying again.

Compost additives

There are various types of compost additives. Some useful traditional ones such as perlite and vermiculite both improve structure and water-holding capacity. Super-absorbent polymers, which are becoming popular, are crystals or gels that absorb and hold water so that it remains available for a longer period. This is potentially a great benefit for plants in containers, but in reality you will still have to treat watering as a daily chore during the summer. If you want to prevent the compost drying out, some kind of automatic watering system is a better – but more costly – solution (see page 106).

PLANTING

Planting is easily taken for granted. It is such an ordinary task that gardeners perform it almost automatically. But there are basic rules always worth repeating, and tips that make some of the trickier tasks easier.

A drainage layer is necessary not only to aid free drainage but also to prevent the compost being washed out through the drainage holes. Traditionally broken clay pots were used, but few of us have enough of these in this age of plastic. Alternatives are coarse gravel, broken polystyrene tiles, or even coarsely chipped bark if the holes are not too large.

Fill the container with an appropriate compost (see page 103), but leave about 2.5 cm (1 in) between compost and rim to make watering easier.

Always water the plants thoroughly about an hour before planting, then arrange them on the surface of the compost – minor adjustments are usually necessary and this is much easier before they have been planted.

Plant deeply enough to cover the root-ball with fresh compost. If part of the root-ball is exposed above the surface it will tend to dry out.

If planting a large shrub or small tree, tease out a few of the roots before planting if they have become very coiled around the inside of the pot.

Plant trailers at a slight angle so that they are already starting to cascade over the edge of the container.

Hanging baskets

Hanging baskets with solid sides are planted like any other container, but be sure to angle the root-ball of cascaders like trailing fuchsias and ivy-leaved geraniums so that they tumble over the edge more readily.

Wire baskets can be planted through the sides (Fig. 15). If yours has a flat base, simply stand it on a table to work on; if it has a rounded base, support it on a bucket or large pot.

Place a thick layer of sphagnum moss, still the most acceptable liner, in the base, then place a small dish or saucer on it to retain some water and reduce drips before adding compost to the level of the first row of plants. After inserting the plants add more moss and compost, and repeat the process until the top is reached. Plant the central plant in the top first, then the main cascaders, finishing off with in-fill plants. Cover the surface with more moss to reduce evaporation and retain moisture.

Black polythene can be used instead of moss. The creases and slits that have to be made for planting will not be visible if the plants do well and completely cover the basket.

To get a big plant through a small hole in the mesh, roll the leaves up in a piece of thin card or stiff paper (like rolling a cigarette). Push the rolled-up tube through the hole, then let the roll unfurl to release the leaves.

WATERING

This tedious chore is the only negative aspect of container gardening. It demands a commitment and simply cannot be neglected. Hanging baskets are the most vulnerable and shrub tubs the least. Windowboxes are also especially vulnerable

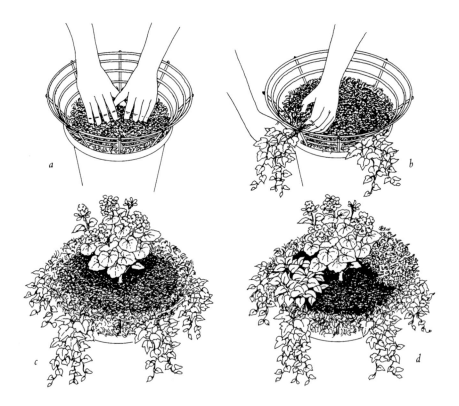

Fig 15 *Planting a hanging basket is easy if you support it on something like a bucket. They look best lined with sphagnum moss, a layer of which should be placed in the bottom before adding a lightweight compost a couple of inches deep (**a**). Insert plants all around the basket at compost height, then add another layer of compost (**b**). Repeat the process once more if the basket is large enough, adding more moss and compost.*

*When filling the top, place a bushy central plant (**c**) first, then a few trailers around the edge. Finally fill the remaining space with compact but bushy plants (**d**).*

to drying out because the wall casts a rain shadow that usually prevents them receiving much moisture even when it rains.

An automatic watering system is the best solution, but these can be expensive and most are designed for greenhouses where the pots are grouped together in a small area. The pipework can be difficult to conceal, but it should not be too conspicuous once the plants have bushed out (Fig. 16). Otherwise minimize the watering chore by grouping most of your plants together in a small area and use a hose on a through-feed hose reel so that getting the hose out and putting it away again can be done with minimum fuss and maximum speed. Various labour-saving gadgets and devices are on the market to help make the watering of hanging baskets less of a problem (Fig. 17), and if you have more than one or two baskets, it is certainly worth trying them out.

Fig 16 *If you have a lot of containers and go away often, some form of automatic watering system is worth the investment. The type sold for watering greenhouse plants can be adapted for this purpose.*

Self-watering windowboxes and troughs are mainly intended for indoor use, but they can be used outdoors if you do not mind the limited range of plastic containers and high cost. Large self-watering floor-standing containers intended for indoors can be used on the patio or balcony, or even in a porch, where their appearance seems more appropriate. Self-watering hanging basket designs are also available (Fig. 18), but they only reduce the frequency of watering slightly and do not eliminate the need for daily care in very hot weather. Unless self-watering containers are large, the reduced amount of compost that they hold can be detrimental.

FERTILIZERS AND FEEDING

Conscientious watering will keep your plants alive and ensure at least a respectable display. Feeding is what will make it spectacular, with lush healthy plants full of vitality and colour.

All container plants need feeding, but some more than others.

Peat-based and peat-substitute composts generally require feeding within a month of planting, though some may contain slow-release fertilizers that sustain growth for longer. Shrubs in a loam-based compost only require an additional liquid boost if they are beginning to look sickly, otherwise a once-a-year application of a general garden fertilizer such as Growmore, or better still a slow-release fertilizer, gently forked into the surface at the beginning of the growing year is often adequate.

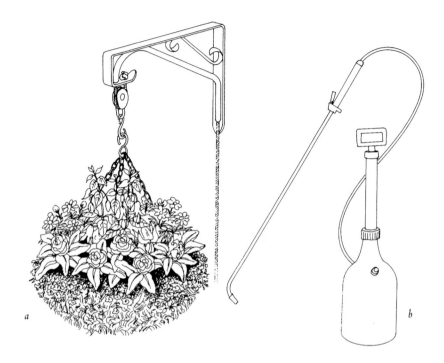

Fig 17 *Watering a hanging basket can be a messy job. Pulley devices that make it easy to lower the basket for watering are particular useful (**a**). Pump-action sprayers with a long lance to reach baskets are available, as well as extension lances for normal compression sprayers (**b**).*

Regular liquid feeding generally produces the best displays, but if you find it difficult to remember to do it, use a slow-release fertilizer that will last for months. These can be mixed into the compost before planting. Some are available in sachets that are placed under the root-ball when you plant.

PRUNING AND GROOMING

Trees and shrubs generally require minimal pruning in tubs because their growth is restricted anyway, but go over them once a year to improve their shape if necessary. At the same time take the opportunity to cut out any all-green shoots on variegated plants (do not wait for this annual check if you notice any all-green shoots earlier).

Dead-heading will generally keep flowers blooming for weeks longer than they would otherwise, and it visually improves the appearance of plants like African marigolds, whose dead blooms are very conspicuous and often start to rot on the plant. Some plants benefit from dead-heading more than others (pansies, petunias and mimulus are examples). With very small, continuous-flowering types such as lobelia it is not practical.

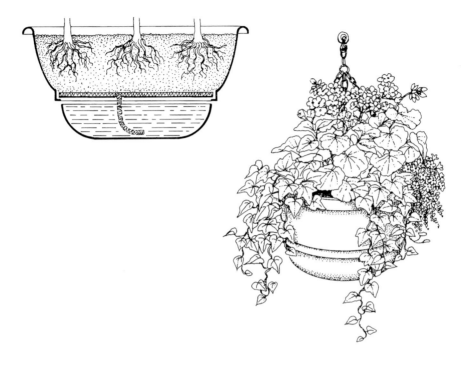

Fig 18 *Several proprietary self-watering baskets are available, but you sacrifice the ability to plant in the sides, and there is less room for compost. They are worth considering if you often have to leave your baskets unattended during the summer.*

KEEPING PLANTS HEALTHY

Plants packed closely together are especially prone to pests and diseases, so keep a close watch for early signs of trouble. Quick action is the key to good control.

It is easy to put off mixing and using insecticides and fungicides if you have to dilute them and require only a very small amount. Ready-mixed sprays (usually sold in small pump type sprayers) are an expensive way of buying garden chemicals litre-for-litre, but you will probably use less because they are so easy and instant to apply that you are more likely to use them to control problems on isolated plants before they spread to others.

Organic pesticides are available, but the simple expedient of picking off affected leaves at the first sign of trouble may be enough to control most problems.

WINTER PROTECTION

Protect your investment in the more tender and exotic plants by making sure winter losses are kept to the minimum.

If you have a conservatory or greenhouse that can be kept frost-proof this is

Ornamental cabbages are as bright as many flowers and will remain attractive for many weeks. They are at their best in the autumn. Cape heathers provide additional autumn colour, and will last into the winter.

the ideal solution provided the plants can be moved easily. For a lot of large plants that need moving twice a year, make a small low trolley on castors. It will remove most of the effort other than that involved in sliding the tubs on and off the trolley.

Vulnerable plants that have to be left out can often be helped to survive and thrive by a few simple precautions. Protection does not look elegant, but it is a price you have to pay.

If possible, plunge the pot in the ground to insulate the roots, then mulch thickly and protect top growth by tying straw or dried bracken around the shoots. This is not practical for evergreens, which will have to make do with a sheet of polythene. It is often winds that do most damage to vulnerable evergreens in winter. Insert three or four canes to the height of the plant, and fix clear polythene around these. If wind damage is the main potential problem leave the top open. If the plants are also likely to be damaged by cold, enclose the top too by taping polythene to the top so that it forms a kind of tent around the plant. Wrap the container with several layers of bubble polythene to provide some insulation for the roots.

Pipe lagging can be used to insulate the stems of palms and other vulnerable plants with a clear trunk.

Do not forget that *empty* terracotta containers may need protection too. If there is any doubt about them being frostproof, keep them dry in a shed or greenhouse.

CHAPTER 9

PLANT PROFILES
AN A–Z OF CONTAINER PLANTS

NO BOOK CAN contain a fully comprehensive list of plants, and this is no exception. Space restraints have meant that some popular plants like dwarf antirrhinums, lilies and zinnias are not included, nor some of the less common container plants for which I have a special affection . . . such as the azure blue trailer *Scaevola aemula* (a great basket plant). This book is about getting the best from containers the year round, and stimulating the clever and creative use of common and uncommon plants alike, so the 150-plus plant profile entries in this chapter have been selected to represent a cross-section of what can be used in containers.

There are thousands of other plants that could be used successfully, and for the adventurous there is always scope for experimentation. But bear in mind that the mainstay of any worthwhile collection of container plants should be mainly those tried and tested favourites that continue to be grown because they are dependable. A whole season can be lost by an inappropriate choice of plants, and a sense of adventure is best cultivated once a framework of really reliable and showy plants has been achieved. Trees and specimen shrubs, in particular, take at least a couple of years to make a real contribution to the container garden, and most of us want some instant colour and interest in the meantime. Some less common kinds have been included, however, as one of the joys of container gardening is the discovery of some plant, or grouping of plants, that works really well in a particular situation.

Alpines have a lot to contribute, especially in sink gardens, but only a handful of the most popular have been included in this A–Z section . . . a visit to the alpine section of any garden centre will provide many more ideas.

HOW TO USE THE PLANT DIRECTORY

Botanists are always changing plant names (sometimes because an earlier published name is the valid one, or because genera and species are redefined in the light of research and expert opinion), but some names changed 30 years ago have not yet fully superseded the old ones in commercial and garden usage. It will probably be a long time before we go into a florist to ask for a bunch of dendranthema instead of chrysanthemums, or look for *Sedum* 'Autumn Joy' in garden centres under its German name 'Herbstfreude', as some would have us do. In a few cases, however, the botanically correct name has been adopted more readily, and the marguerites that we have known for years as *Chrysanthemum frutescens* are now often sold in garden centres as argyranthemums. In this book a pragmatic approach has been adopted, and the plants will be found under the names by which they are most often sold. If an alternative name is commonly used, this has been cross-referenced.

Widely used common names have been included, and cross-referenced to their Latin name.

KEY TO SYMBOLS

TYPE OF PLANT		MOST SUITABLE USES	
Al	Alpine	**Hg**	Hanging basket
Bi	Biennial		
Bu	Bulb	**Tr**	Trough
Cl	Climber	**Tu**	Tub
Ev	Evergreen	**Ur**	Urn
Gr	Grass or grass-like plant	**Wb**	Window-box
Ha	Hardy annual		
Hb	Herbaceous		
Hha	Half-hardy annual (tender)	BEST POSITION	
		○	Full sun
Sb	Shrub	◑	Partial shade
Sc	Succulent	●	Full shade
Te	Tree		
Pr	Not fully hardy, needs winter protection		

Abutilon megapotamicum
Sb, Pr, ○, Tu
Distinctive yellow and red pendent flowers throughout summer. *A.m.* 'Variegatum' has the bonus of leaves mottled yellow. Height: 1.8 m (6 ft).
USE Creates an unusual and exotic effect against a sunny wall.
GROWING TIPS Train against a wall. Insulate pot in winter in cold areas.

Acanthus Bear's breeches
Hb, ○/◑, Tu
A. mollis forms a clump of large, deeply lobed foliage. Imposing spikes of white and purple hooded tubular flowers in mid and late summer. Leaves persist for a long time in autumn. *A. spinosus* has more deeply divided, spine-tipped leaves. Height: 90 cm (3 ft).
USE Specimen plant in a large tub as a focal point.
GROWING TIP Feed monthly throughout the summer.

Acer palmatum Japanese maple
Sb/Te, ○/◑, Tu
Shrub or small tree with bright green lobed leaves, finely divided in 'Dissectum'. The purple-leaved 'Dissectum Atropurpureum' is widely grown.
USE Specimen plant to produce an atmosphere of elegance.
GROWING TIP Cold winds can cause the newly emerging leaves to shrivel as they unfurl in spring. Needs a protected, sheltered site.

Acorus gramineus 'Wogon'
Gr, Ev, ○, Tr/Wb
Golden grass-like leaves. Tufted habit. Height: 15 cm (6 in).
USES Best in container planted for year-round interest.
GROWING TIPS Is slow-growing so avoid planting with very vigorous plants. The almost black *Ophiopogon planiscapus nigrescens* is a good companion.

Aeonium arboreum
Sc, Pr, Ev, ○, Tr/Tu
A shrubby succulent, each stem crowned with a rosette of shiny green leaves (dark purple on 'Atropurpureum'). Height: 60 cm (2 ft).
USE Grow among other large succulents such as agaves, or with alpines.

GROWING TIP Best taken indoors for the winter, except in very mild areas.

African lily, see *Agapanthus*

African marigold, see *Tagetes erecta*

Agapanthus African lily
Hb, Ev, ○/◑/●, Tu
Rounded heads of blue or white flowers, mid to late summer. 'Headbourne Hybrids' are hardier than most. In mild areas try *A. campanulatus, A. orientalis* and *A. praecox* (syn. *A. umbellatus*). Height: 75 cm (2½ ft).
USES Excellent tub plant. Makes a splendid focal point.
GROWING TIPS Leave undisturbed to form a large clump. In cold areas take into a greenhouse or conservatory for the winter. In mild areas insulate the container even if those in beds and borders normally survive.

Agave americana
'Variegata' Century plant
Sc, Pr, Ev, ○, Tu/Ur
Large strap-like leaves edged yellow. Height: 45 cm (1½ ft).
USES Use as a focal point plant, small ones in urns or small pots, large ones in bigger tubs.
GROWING TIP Even in very favourable districts overwintering outside is unreliable. Move to a frost-proof greenhouse or conservatory for the winter.

Ageratum houstonianum Floss flower
Hha, ○, Tr/Wb
Masses of small powder-puff like blue flowers (also whites and pinks). Choose compact varieties for containers. Height: 15–25 cm (6–10 in).

SE Use to break up the more vivid
colours of mixed bedding.
ROWING TIP Pick off dead flower heads,
which turn brown with age.

Ajuga reptans Bugle
Ib, ○/◑, Hg/Tr/Wb
A carpeting plant with small spikes of blue
flowers, but grown mainly for variously
coloured and variegated foliage. Height:
10 cm (4 in) (in flower).
SES Ground cover around base of trees
and shrubs in tubs, and for front of a
permanently planted windowbox. Foliage
effect in a summer basket.

Alchemilla mollis Lady's mantle
Ib, ○/◑, Tr/Tu
Rounded, fresh green foliage, sprays of
tiny greenish-yellow flowers in summer.
Height: 50 cm (20 in).
USES Ground cover for deciduous trees in
large tubs. Contrasts well with purple
foliage plants such as *Acer palmatum
Dissectum Atropurpureum*'.
ROWING TIP Deadhead

Algerian iris, see *Iris unguicularis*

Allium albopilosum
Bu, ○, Tr/Tu
Pretty 15 cm (6 in) wide heads of star-
shaped pink flowers in early summer. Also
sold as *A. christophii*. Height: 45 cm
(18 in).

A. christophii see *A. albopilosum*

Alyssum maritimum Sweet alyssum
Ha, ○/◑, Hg/Tr/Wb
Low, mound-forming plant with small
and slightly fragrant flowers that bloom
for months. White is the most popular
colour but there are lilac-pinks and
purples. Height: 8–10 cm (3–4 in).
USES As an edging (often used with
lobelia) for troughs and windowboxes.
Also useful for filling in the sides of
hanging baskets.
GROWING TIP Do not grow with large,
vigorous plants that will swamp them.

Alyssum saxatile Gold dust
Al, Ev, ○, Tr/Tu/Wb
Masses of small bright yellow flowers in
late spring and early summer. Grey-green
foliage. There are varieties with pale
yellow flowers. Height: 20 cm (8 in).

USES Spring windowboxes. Ground
cover around deciduous shrubs.

Amaranthus caudatus Love-lies-
bleeding
Hha, ○, Tu/Wb
Long red tassel flowers (green in the
variety 'Viridis') in summer. Height:
60–75 cm (2–2½ ft).
USES As a centrepiece in a tub of colourful
summer bedding, or on its own in a vase
or urn on a pedestal, where the long tassels
can tumble down.
GROWING TIP Avoid a windy position,
which can damage the tassels.

Amelanchier Snowy mespilus
Sb/Te, ○/◑, Tu
A. canadensis and *A. lamarckii* are multi-
stemmed shrubs or small single-stemmed
trees with masses of white flowers in late
spring and good autumn leaf colour.
Height: 2.4 m (8 ft).
USE Grow in a large tub as a dual-interest
patio plant.
GROWING TIP Feed in spring.

Anchusa capensis
Ha, ○, Tr/Wb
A hardy biennial but the varieties sold are
best grown as annuals. 'Dawn' is a pretty
mixture with shades of lavender, pink,
blue and white flowers. Height: 23 cm
(9 in).
USE Best grown in a box on its own,
sown directly into the container.
GROWING TIPS Sow a packet of anchusa
directly into the compost. Keep the box in
a light place, thin surplus seedlings if too
many germinate.

Anemone blanda
Bu, ○/◑, Tu/Wb
Daisy-like flowers over feathery foliage on
compact plants. Blue, pink, red and white
varieties are available. Height: 10 cm
(4 in).
USE Attractive around the base of a
deciduous tree in a large tub.
GROWING TIP Soak tubers for a few
hours before planting.

Anemone nemorosa Wood anemone
Bu, ◑/●, Tu/Wb
Daisy-like white flowers, ferny foliage.
Height: 15 cm (6 in).
USES AND GROWING TIPS As *A. blanda*.

Angelica tree, see *Aralia elata*

Aralia elata Angelica tree
Te, ○/◑, Tu
Tree grown for foliage effect. Large,
divided leaves, bordered yellow in
'Aureovariegata', creamy white in
'Variegata'. Height: 2.4 m (8 ft).
USE Specimen plant useful as a focal
point.
GROWING TIP Shelter from strong
winds.

**Argyranthemum frutescens, see
*Chrysanthemum frutescens***

Armeria maritima Thrift
Al, Ev, ○, Wb
Tufts of evergreen grass-like foliage. Small
drumstick balls of pink, red or white
flowers in late spring and early summer.
Height: 10 cm (4 in).
USES Permanently planted windowbox.
Good for coastal areas.
GROWING TIPS Ensure good drainage.
Do not over-feed.

Arundinaria Bamboo
Gr, Ev, ○/◑, Tu
Several grass-like bamboos, some with
typical bamboo canes, are suitable for
containers. Two of the best are *A. murielae*
(dark green, elegant leaves; 1.5 m (5 ft))
and *A. viridistriata* (bright gold and green;
60 cm (2 ft)).
USE Specimen patio plants in oriental
containers.
GROWING TIPS Add extra organic matter
to the compost. Keep very moist.

Asplenium scolopendrium, see Ferns

Athyrium filix-femina, see Ferns

Astilbe
Hb, ○/◑, Tr/Tu
Feathery pink, red or white plumes above
attractive, divided foliage. Choose from
the many hybrids for a large container, use
dwarfs such as *A. chinensis pumila* (pink,
23 cm (9 in)) in a small container. Height:
60 cm (2 ft).
USES Permanently planted trough or tub.
GROWING TIP Never allow the compost
to dry out. Keep moist.

Agapanthus *'Headbourne Hybrids'*.

Aubrieta deltoidea
Al, Ev, ○, Tr/Wb
Forms a carpet of blue, purple, carmine
flowers in spring. Height: 5 cm (2 in).
USES Spring interest and permanently
planted troughs and windowboxes.
GROWING TIP Cut back after flowering
to keep compact.

Aucuba japonica Spotted laurel
Sb, Ev, ○/◑/●, Tr/Tu
Glossy-leaved evergreen. Variegated
forms are usually grown. Female varieties,
such as 'Variegata', may have red berries.
Height: 1.5 m (5 ft).
USE Good for a shady area.
GROWING TIP For berries grow two; one
male, one female.

Autumn crocus, see *Colchichum* and
Crocus

Bamboo, see *Arundinaria*

Bay, see *Laurus nobilis*

Bear's breeches, see *Acanthus*

Begonia semperflorens Fibrous-rooted
begonia
Hha, ○/◑/●, Hg/Tr/Wb

Compact plants with green, bronze or
purple-red foliage, and masses of small
red, pink or white flowers all summer.
Height: 15–23 cm (6–9 in).
USES Best in a massed display. Good for
single-subject planting.
GROWING TIPS Add extra organic
material to the compost. Keep moist.

Begonia, Tuberous
Hha/Bu, ○/◑, Hg/Tr/Tu/Wb
Large double or semi-double flowers in
shades of red, pink, yellow and white.
Pendulous types are grown from tubers.
Most upright types, such as the Non-stop
range, are now grown from seed. Height:
30 cm (12 in).
USES Pendulous types: baskets. Others:
tubs, troughs, windowboxes.

Bellis perennis Double daisy
Bi, ○/◑, Tr/Tu/Wb
Large double daisies, some like pompoms.
Shades of red, pink and white. Height:
10–15 cm (4–6 in).
USES Mix with spring bulbs. Use around
deciduous trees for spring colour.
GROWING TIP Deadhead regularly.

Bergenia cordifolia Elephants' ears
Hb, Ev, ○/◑/●, Tr/Wb
Large leaves, purplish in winter. Pink
flowers in spring. Height: 45 cm (1½ ft).
USES Evergreen colour in permanent
plantings.
GROWING TIP Divide when they
outgrow their space.

Black-eyed Susan, see *Thunbergia*
alata

Bluebell, see *Endymion non-scriptus*

Bowles' golden grass, see *Milium*
effusum aureum

Box, see *Buxus sempervirens*

Brachycome iberidifolia Swan River
daisy
Hha, ○, Hg/Wb
Carpet of blue daisy-type flowers. Height:
30 cm (12 in).
USES Baskets, windowboxes, mixed or
alone. Good with pelargoniums.
GROWING TIP Pinch out tips when plants
are small to encourage bushiness.

Chrysanthemum *(Argyranthemum) frutescens 'Sharpitor'*.

Brassica oleracea Ornamental cabbage
Ha, ○/◑, Tr/Wb
Typical cabbage shape but leaves variegated pink, red, purple, white. Ornamental kale is similar but the leaves are more divided. Height: 30 cm (12 in).
USE Grow them to provide autumn interest after summer bedding plants.
GROWING TIP Pick off any caterpillars before they damage the leaves.

Buddleia davidii Butterfly bush
Sb, ○/◑, Tu
Long spikes of blue, purple, crimson, white flowers in summer and autumn. Very attractive to butterflies. Height: 2.4 m (8 ft).
USE To attract butterflies to the patio or garden.
GROWING TIP Prune hard each spring to prevent leggy growth.

Bugle, see *Ajuga reptans*

Butterfly bush, see *Buddleia davidii*

Busy Lizzie, see *Impatiens*

Buxus sempervirens Box
Sb, Ev, ○/◑/●, Tu

Small evergreen leaves, easily clipped to a formal shape. 'Suffruticosa' is the dwarf box, only 30 cm (12 in). There are variegated forms of the taller kinds, and these are slightly brighter plants. Height: 1.5 m (5 ft).
USE Best clipped to formal and decorative shapes.
GROWING TIP Clip twice a year to maintain a neat shape.

Cabbage, ornamental, see *Brassica oleracea*

Calceolaria rugosa
Hha, ○/◑, Hg/Wb
Clusters of yellow pouch-shaped flowers in summer. Height: 25 cm (10 in).
USES Mix with bedding for splashes of yellow. Good on own in basket.
GROWING TIP Deadhead regularly.

Calendula Pot marigold
Ha, ○, Tr
Large (usually) double flowers in shades of yellow and orange. For containers choose a very dwarf variety such as 'Fiesta Gitana', 30 cm (12 in).

USES A cheap and cheerful source of colour. Can be sown direct.
GROWING TIP Watch out for mildew on the leaves.

Calluna vulgaris Scotch heather
Sb, Ev, ○/◑, Tr/Wb
Well-known evergreen shrublet. Many varieties, some with gold or reddish foliage. Late summer/autumn flowers. Height: 20–60 cm (8–24 in).
USE Plant in year-round containers.
GROWING TIP Not lime-tolerant. Use ericaceous compost if possible.

Camellia
Sb, Ev, ◑, Tu
Beautiful, large spring blooms, in shades of pink, red and white, set against attractive glossy, evergreen foliage. Many varieties, including singles and doubles, flowering between mid winter and mid spring. Height: 1.8 m (6 ft).
USE Specimen plants in large containers.
GROWING TIPS Use an ericaceous compost. Best in dappled shade.

Campanula carpatica
Al, ○/◑, Wb

Blue or white upward-facing bell flowers in summer. Height: 23 cm (9 in).
USES Permanently planted windowbox. Alpine windowbox. Often sold in flower as a pot plant, and useful for filling in gaps left by other plants.
GROWING TIP Buy as a flowering pot-plant to use for instant effect.

Candytuft, see *Iberis umbellata*

Canna Indian shot
Hb, Pr, ○/◑, Tu
Lance-shaped leaves, often flushed purple or copper. Spikes of flowers in colours that include red, orange, pink and yellow. Height: 90 cm (3 ft).
USES Centrepiece for mixed summer bedding. Alone for 'tropical' effect.
GROWING TIPS Store rhizomes in frost-free place. Avoid windy site.

Cape heather, see *Erica gracilis* and *E. hyemalis*

Castor oil plant, see *Ricinus communis*

Castor oil plant, false, see *Fatsia japonica*

Ceratostigma willmottianum Hardy plumbago
Sb, ○, Tr
Small blue flowers summer and autumn. Autumn tints. Height: 60 cm (2 ft).
USE Permanent planting of shrubs or herbaceous plants.
GROWING TIP Best in a sunny, sheltered position.

***Chamaecyparis communis* 'Sentinel', see Conifers**

***Chamaecyparis lawsoniana* 'Ellwoodii', see Conifers**

***Chamaecyparis pisifera* 'Boulevard' and 'Filifera Aurea', see Conifers**

Chamaerops humilis Dwarf fan palm
Sb, Pr, Ev, ○, Tu
Palm with large, fan-like foliage. Height: 1.2 m (4 ft).
USE Focal point or to create a 'tropical' effect on a patio.
GROWING TIP In mild areas protect outdoors; best brought in for winter.

Cheiranthus Wallflower
Bi, ○/◑, Tr/Tu/Wb
Well-known fragrant spring-flowering plants. Available as separate colours or as mixtures. Choose dwarf varieties, 30 cm (12 in), for containers. Siberian wallflowers (*C. × allionii*) flower a little later and are yellow or orange.
USE Place near the door or where the fragrance can be appreciated.
GROWING TIP Pinch out growing tips while young to encourage bushiness. Wall flowers will grow in a shady place but the plants will be taller and the flowers fewer.

Chilean glory flower, see *Eccremocarpus scaber*

Chimonanthus praecox Wintersweet
Sb, ○, Tu
Fragrant yellow flowers on bare stems in winter. Also sold as *C. fragrans*. Height: 2.4 m (8 ft).
USE Tub, where winter flowers can be appreciated.
GROWING TIP Best in a sunny, sheltered position.

Choisya ternata Mexican orange blossom
Sb, Ev, ○/◑/●, Tu
Pleasant aromatic evergreen foliage ('Sundance' is gold), white flowers in late spring. Height: 1.5 m (5 ft).
USE Ideal tub plant for a patio.
GROWING TIP Avoid a windy position.

Christmas rose, see *Helleborus niger*

Chrysanthemum
Hb, ○/◑, Tr/Wb
Masses of daisy-type flowers in many colours. Of the many types available the dwarf Korean chrysanthemums, 60 cm (2 ft) are useful for autumn colour in troughs. All-year-round pot chrysanthemums (which are specially treated and dwarfed) can be bought at any time of the year to provide instant colour. *Chrysanthemum frutescens*, the marguerite, also now often sold under its more recent name of *Argyranthemum frutescens*, is an invaluable summer-flowering container plant with white, yellow, or pink daisy-type flowers. Heights vary with type of plant and method of cultivation.

USES Marguerites in bush form are ideal for windowboxes or troughs; grown as standards they make good tub plants. Other types are best in troughs or windowboxes, especially for autumn interest.
GROWING TIPS Discard year-round pot chrysanthemums when they have finished flowering. Overwinter Korean chrysanthemums and marguerites in a cool, frost-free place and take cuttings in late winter.

Cineraria maritima
Hha, ○/◑, Tr/Wb
Usually sold under this name in seed catalogues, but may be listed as *Senecio bicolor*. Silver-leaved perennial foliage plant usually treated as a half-hardy annual. Height: 30 cm (12 in).
USES As a contrast plant in mixed summer bedding. Usually used in window boxes and troughs, but can be effective in a basket.
GROWING TIP Pinch out any flower buds that appear.

Clematis viticella
Sb/Cl, ○, Tu
Typical clematis flowers from mid summer to autumn. Height: 2.4 m (8 ft).
USE Climber to place against a trellis to add interest to a wall.
GROWING TIP Prune to within 60 cm (2 ft) of base in late winter.

Colchicum Autumn crocus
Bu, ○/◑/●, Tr/Tu/Wb
Big crocus-shaped pink, lilac or white flowers (some double). Popular species are *C. autumnale* and *C. speciosum*. Height (in flower): 15 cm (6 in).
USE Pockets of autumn colour among permanent plantings.
GROWING TIP Do not plant where the tall leaves hide other plants in spring.

Coleus blumei Flame nettle
Hha, ○/◑, Hg/Tr
Brilliantly coloured and variegated leaves. 'Poncho' has a cascading habit.
USES Cascading type as single-subject planting in a basket. Mixed boxes.
GROWING TIPS Pick off any flower spikes that appear. Avoid a windy spot.

Conifers
○/◑, Tu/Tr/Wb

Most dwarf and slow-growing conifers are suitable for containers . . . at least for a couple of years before being planted in the garden. Garden centres often have hundreds to choose from, but the following are worth looking for: *Chamaecyparis lawsoniana* 'Ellwoodii' (pyramidal, grey-green); *Chamaecyparis pisifera* 'Boulevard' (pyramidal, silver-blue), *C. p.* 'Filifera Aurea' (dome-shaped, thread-like golden foliage); *Juniperus communis* 'Sentinel' (narrow column, green); *Juniperus horizontalis* 'Glauca' (prostrate, blue-green); *Juniperus × media* 'Blaauw' (stiffly angled branches, blue-grey), *J × m.* 'Mint Julep' (semi-prostrate, arching, green); *Juniperus squamata* 'Blue Star' (bushy, steel blue); *Taxus baccata* 'Fastigiata Robusta' (narrow column, dark green); *Thuja occidentalis* 'Rheingold' (pyramidal, gold); *Thuja orientalis* 'Aurea Nana' (oval, golden).
USES Best in groups of contrasting shapes and colours. Can also be mixed with dwarf shrubs in permanent plantings.
GROWING TIP Some are sensitive to dry roots; do not neglect watering.

Convolvulus
Ha/Cl, ○, Tr

Bindweed-like flowers, but in shades of blue and pink as well as white. *C. major* is a climber to 1.8 m (6 ft), *C. minor* remains compact at 30 cm (12 in).
USE Plant in a trough, supporting *C. major* with a trellis.
GROWING TIP Deadhead regularly.

Cordyline australis Cabbage palm
Sb, Pr, Ev, ○, Tu

Rosette of lance-shaped leaves when young, then develops a trunk and resembles a palm tree. *C.a. purpurea* is a coppery purple. Height: 1.8 m (6 ft).
USES Focal point plant in a tub. Tolerates coastal conditions well.
GROWING TIPS Take in young plants for the winter. Older ones can be left outside in mild areas, but insulate the trunk with pipe lagging.

Cortaderia selloana 'Pumila' Dwarf
pampas grass
Gr, Ev, ○/◑, Tu

Clump of grassy leaves. White flower plumes in autumn. Height: 1.2 m (4 ft).
USES Specimen plant in tub. Do not mix with other plants.
GROWING TIP Cut down the plant each spring before new growth starts.

Cotoneaster horizontalis Fishbone
cotoneaster
Sb, ○/◑, Tr/Tu

Small white flowers in summer. Red berries/leaf tints in autumn. Spreading.
USES As a trailer in a trough or tub. If placed against wall will grow upwards.
GROWING TIP Prune to shape only if necessary.

Cotoneaster 'Hybridus Pendulus'
Te, ○/◑, Tu

Small weeping tree as a grafted standard, grown for berries. Height: 1.8 m (6 ft).
USES Specimen patio plant. Try planting a prostrate cotoneaster around the base, for an even more striking effect.
GROWING TIP Prune to shape only if necessary.

Cotton lavender, see Santolina chamaecyparissus

Crab apple, see Malus floribunda

Creeping Jenny, see Lysimachia nummularia

Crocus
Bu, ○, Tr/Wb

Crocuses need no introduction. The large-flowered Dutch hybrids are widely planted, but try the following too: *C. chrysanthus* (smaller, late winter and early spring, various colours), *C. laevigatus* (mid autumn to early winter, pale lavender to white), *C. sativus* (mid autumn, purple), *C. speciosus* (mid autumn, pale blue or white), *C. tommasinianus* (late winter and early spring, pale mauve), *C. zonatus* (syn. *C. kotschyanus*, early and mid autumn, lilac-blue).
USES Mixed bulb displays and to fill gaps in permanent plantings.
GROWING TIP Plant some corms in pots to fill in gaps in mixed plantings.

Curry plant, see Helichrysum angustifolium

Cyclamen coum
Bu, ◑/●, Tr/Tu

Cyclamen-shaped pink, carmine or white flowers in winter. Height: 8 cm (3 in).
USE Winter-interest around base of trees and shrubs.
GROWING TIP Leave undisturbed if possible.

Dahlia
Bu, Pr, ○, Tr/Wb

Dahlias come in many shapes and sizes, from miniature to giants of 1.2 m (4 ft) or more with flowers 25 cm (10 in) across, and in most shades except blue. For containers, choose dwarfs such as the Lilliput range.
USE Best for single-subject planting, especially for late colour.
GROWING TIP Lift and store tubers in frost-free place for next year.

Daffodil, see Narcissus

Datura Angel's trumpet
Sb, Pr, Ev, ○/◑, Tu

Huge trumpet-like pendulous flowers all summer. 'Grand Marnier' is peach, *D. suaveolens* white, *D. cornigera* a double white. 2.1 m (7 ft).
USE Specimen plant to create a tropical atmosphere.
GROWING TIPS Needs sheltered position. Overwinter in a frost-proof place.

Dianthus Pink, carnation
Hb, Ev, ○, Tr/Wb

Modern pinks have fragrant double flowers and grey foliage. Trailing carnations may have green foliage. Height: 30 cm (12 in).
USES Modern pinks such as 'Doris' (pink, fragrant), with a long flowering season, are useful for permanent plantings. Use trailing carnations for single-subject planting in a windowbox.
GROWING TIPS Deadhead. Watch for leaf miner in the leaves.

Dianthus barbatus Sweet William
Bi, ○, Tr

Flat heads of fragrant flowers in reds, pinks, white. Height: 30–45 cm (12–18 in).
USE Single-subject planting, for early summer interest.

Cordyline australis purpurea *surrounded by* Philadelphus coronarius *'Aureus'.*

GROWING TIP Grow in nursery bed until ready for planting in autumn.

Diascia cordata
Hb, ○/◑, Tr/Tu/Ur/Wb
Clusters of pink flowers and small heart-shaped leaves. Height: 15 cm (6 in).
USES Let it trail over the edge of a windowbox or urn in a mixed planting.
GROWING TIPS Pinch out tips of young plants to encourage bushiness. Deadhead.

Double daisy, see *Bellis perennis*

***Dryopteris filix-mas*, see Ferns**

Eccremocarpus scaber Chilean glory flower
Hha, Cl, ○/◑, Tr/Tu
Small yellow, orange or red tubular flowers. Height: 2.1 m (7 ft).
USE Cover for a sheltered wall. Provide trellis support.
GROWING TIP A perennial, but except in very mild areas grow as annual.

Elaeagnus pungens 'Maculata'
Sb, Ev, ○/◑, Tu
Very striking year-round yellow and green

foliage. Height: 1.8 m (6 ft).
USES Winter interest or to screen a dull wall.
GROWING TIP Cut out any all-green shoots that appear.

Elephants' ears, see *Bergenia cordifolia*

Endymion non-scriptus Bluebell
Bu, ◑/●, Tr/Tu
Large version of the wild bluebell – pink, white, blue. Height: 30 cm (12 in).
USE Around base of trees and shrubs.
GROWING TIP Leave undisturbed if possible.

Eranthis hyemalis Winter aconite
Bu, ○/◑/●, Tr/Tu/Wb
Yellow, buttercup flowers with green ruff in late winter. Height: 8 cm (3 in).
USE Brings early colour to a permanently planted container.
GROWING TIP Flowers best if left undisturbed to form established clumps.

Erica Heather
Sb, Ev, ○, Tr/Tu
Heathers need no introduction. *E. carnea*

and *E.* × *darleyensis* are both winter-flowering and there are many varieties, some with coloured foliage. Cape heathers (*E. gracilis* and *E. hyemalis*), which are sold as pot-plants in autumn and early winter, are not hardy but can be used to provide many weeks of colour before being discarded.
USES Winter interest and permanently planted troughs and windowboxes.
GROWING TIP Deadhead with shears or secateurs once flowering is over.

Euonymus fortunei
Sb, Ev, ○/◑/●, Tr/Tu/Wb
Versatile foliage plants with small but colourful leaves. Two popular varieties are 'Emerald 'n' Gold' (green and gold) and 'Emerald Gaiety' (silver, gold and green). Height: 30 cm (12 in), but will climb up a wall.
USES Ground cover around shrubs or trees in tubs. Edging to tumble over the edge of shrub windowboxes or troughs.
GROWING TIP Can be trained upwards if container is against a wall.

Fan palm, see *Trachycarpus fortunei*

Fuchsias will make large specimens if overwintered in a conservatory.

Fatsia japonica False castor oil plant
Sb, Ev, ○ / ◑ / ●, Tr/Tu
Large hand-shaped leaves. 'Variegata' has
creamy margins. Height: 1.5 m (5 ft).
USES In mixed shrub troughs when
young. As specimen plant in tub later.
GROWING TIP Grow 'Variegata' in a
sheltered position.

Felicia amelloides
Hb, ○, Hg/Wb
Intense blue small daisy-type flowers.
Height: 25 cm (10 in).
USES Mix with other summer bedding or
use for single-subject planting.
GROWING TIP Hardy in very mild areas,
otherwise treat as an annual.

Ferns
Hb, ○ / ◑, Tr
Ferns are generally best grouped together
as part of a foliage trough for a shady
corner. Suitable ferns are *Athyrium filix-
femina*, lady fern, delicate feathery fronds,
60 cm (2 ft); *Phyllitis scolopendrium*, syn.
Asplenium scolopendrium, hart's-tongue
fern, undivided leaves, 30 cm (12 in);
Dryopteris filix-mas, male fern, deep green

lobed fronds, 60 cm (2 ft); *Matteuccia
struthiopteris*, shuttlecock fern, rosette of
tall, plume-like foliage resembling a
shuttlecock, 90 cm (3 ft).
USE Foliage effect in a shady corner.
GROWING TIP Make sure they do not go
short of water in summer.

Forget-me-not, see *Myosotis*

French marigold, see *Tagetes patula*

Fuchsia
Sb, Pr, ○, Hg/Tr/Tu/Wb
Fuchsias, with their tubular flowers and
spreading sepals, need no introduction.
There are hundreds of varieties, many of
them with a weeping habit ideal for a
hanging basket. One of the best is
'Cascade'.
USES Plant cascading varieties in hanging
baskets (alone or in a mixed planting) or at
the front of a windowbox. Ordinary
tender varieties are good for tubs, troughs
and windowboxes. 'Tom Thumb' is
useful for a permanently planted shrub
windowbox or trough.
GROWING TIPS Overwinter old plants or

cuttings of tender varieties in a frost-free
place. Pinch out tips of young plants to
encourage bushiness.

Galanthus Snowdrop
Bu, ◑ / ●, Tr/Tu/Wb
The nodding white bells of the common
snowdrop (*G. nivalis*) need no
introduction. *G. caucasicus* flowers earlier.
Height: 15 cm (6 in).
USE Best in permanently planted
containers.
GROWING TIP Leave undisturbed to
make large clumps.

**Geranium (bedding type), see
*Pelargonium***

Glechoma hederacea
'Variegata' Ground ivy
Hb, ○ / ◑ / ◐, Hg/Wb
Long thin trailing stems with small semi-
evergreen white margined leaves.
USE As a long trailer in windowboxes and
baskets.
GROWING TIP Avoid a very windy site.
Strong winds may scorch the leaves.

Grape hyacinth, see *Muscari armeniacum*

Ground ivy, see *Glechoma hederacea* 'Variegata'

Gunnera manicata
Hb, Pr, ○/◑/●, Tu
Huge rhubarb-shaped leaves about 1.5 m (5 ft) across. Height: 1.8 m (6 ft).
USES Focal point plant, or as part of a foliage effect corner.
GROWING TIPS Needs a sheltered spot. Protect *in situ* in winter. Keep well fed and watered.

Hakonechloa macra 'Albo-aurea'
Gr, ○/◑, Tr/Tu
Forms attractive tufts of golden grass foliage. Height: 25 cm (10 in).
USES In a mixed planting to add texture and colour, or in a tub on its own.
GROWING TIP Do not forget to feed.

Hamamelis mollis Witch hazel
Sb, ○/◑, Tu
Spidery-looking fragrant yellow flowers in mid winter. Height: 1.8 m (6 ft).
USE Winter-interest tub, in a position close to a path used in winter.
GROWING TIP Provide a sheltered area.

Hart's-tongue fern, see Ferns

Heather, see *Calluna* and *Erica*

Hebe
Sb, Ev, ○/◑, Tr/Wb
Neat foliage shrubs, some variegated, others with attractive flowers. Many are vulnerable in cold winters but those listed are hardy outdoors in mild areas in most years. *Hebe albicans* 'Red Edge', grey-green leaves edged red, 30 cm (12 in); *H.* 'Autumn Glory', green leaves shaded purple, violet-blue flowers summer to mid autumn, 45 cm (1½ ft); *H. × franciscana* 'Variegata', cream and green leaves, 60 cm (2 ft); *H.* 'Great Orme', bright pink flowers, 75 cm (2½ ft); *H.* 'Marjorie', light violet and white flowers, 75 cm (2½ ft); *H.* 'Midsummer Beauty', green leaves, reddish beneath, lavender-purple flowers all summer, 90 cm (3 ft); *H. pinguifolia* 'Pagei', grey leaves, white flowers, 15 cm (6 in); *H. rakaiensis* (syn. *H. subalpina*), mound of pale green leaves, white flowers

in late spring, 60 cm (2 ft).
USES Small ones in windowboxes, any in year-round shrub displays.
GROWING TIP Overwinter cuttings under protection in case of winter losses.

Hedera helix Ivy
Sb/Cl, Ev, ○/○/●,
Hg/Tr/Tu/Wb ◗
These popular foliage plants are useful as climbers or trailers in all kinds of containers. There are many leaf forms and colours, but small-leaved kinds are generally best for containers. A shortlist of good ones should include: 'Adam' (white-edged), 'Buttercup' (deep yellow), 'Glacier' (grey and green), and 'Goldheart' (splashed yellow).
USES Excellent for trailing over edge of permanently planted containers. Useful for covering wall in courtyard garden.
GROWING TIP Trim back annually if the plant becomes straggly.

Helichrysum angustifolium Curry plant
Sb, Ev, ○, Tr/Tu/Wb
Silver-grey needle-like foliage that smells of curry. Height: 30 cm (12 in).
USE As a 'contrast' shrub in a permanent planting.
GROWING TIPS Cut off any flowers that appear. Trim to shape in spring.

Helichrysum petiolare
Sh, Pr, Ev, ○/◑, Hg/Tu/Wb
Grey-leaved prostrate foliage plant that will also cascade. There is also a pale yellow form, and *H. microphyllum* is like a small-leaved version.
USE Mix with bright summer bedding plants, especially in baskets.
GROWING TIPS Take cuttings in autumn and overwinter in frost-free place.

Heliotrope, see *Heliotropium*

Heliotropium Cherry pie
Sb, Pr, ○/◑, Tr/Wb
Dense clusters of violet-purple flowers. Dark foliage. Height: 38 cm (15 in).
USE With summer bedding, to contrast with brighter colours.
GROWING TIP Tender perennial, but usually grown as a half-hardy annual.

Helleborus Hellebore
Hb, Ev, ◑/●, Tr/Wb
Hellebores are useful for their cup or saucer shaped flowers that generally appear in winter or spring. *H. atrorubens* (plum-purple, mid winter to early spring, deciduous), *H. niger* (Christmas rose, white, mid to late winter). *H. orientalis* (Lenten rose, mainly purples and pinks, late winter and early spring), *H. viridis* (yellowish-green, late winter and early spring, deciduous). Height: 30–60 cm (1–2 ft).

Holly, see *Ilex*

Hosta Plantain lily
Hb, ○/◑/●, Tr/Tu
Popular foliage plants, often variegated. There are dozens of good varieties, large and small, all of which can be used if the container and arrangement is large enough. Variegation often fades as the season progresses.
USE Good for foliage arrangements for a shady spot.
GROWING TIP Use slug bait, or control these pests in some other way.

Houttuynia cordata 'Chameleon'
Hb, ○/◑, Tr/Tu/Wb
Multi-coloured foliage, variegated red, yellow, green. Height: 23 cm (9 in).
USE Most effective as a single-subject planting. A real eyecatcher.
GROWING TIPS Keep moist. Remove any non-variegated shoots.

Hyacinth, see *Hyacinthus*

Hyacinthus Hyacinth
Bu, ○/◑, Tr/Wb
The popular and fragrant hyacinth needs no introduction. For outdoors buy the smaller and cheaper bulbs, but use plenty of them for a good display.
USES As an element in a mixed spring display or for single-subject boxes.
GROWING TIP For garden display, small bulbs are usually satisfactory.

Hydrangea
Sb, ○/◑/●, Tu
The mop-headed Hortensia hydrangeas are best for tubs. Height: 1.2 m (4 ft).
USE Effective specimen plant to grow in half-barrel by the front door.

GROWING TIP Use an ericaceous compost for good blues.

Iberis umbellata Candytuft
Ha, ○/◑, Tr/Wb
Clusters of white, pink, red flowers. Height: 25 cm (10 in).
USES Cheap way to fill a spare windowbox. Use as single subject.
GROWING TIP Sow directly into compost in spring.

Ilex Holly
Sb, Ev, ○/◑/●, Tu
The common green holly with its red berries is known to everyone, but choose a gold and green variety for brightness (some of these do not have berries, so check). Train into a formal shape.
USES Excellent as a formal clipped shrub near front door, or as a focal point.
GROWING TIP Cut out any all-green shoots on variegated varieties as soon as they appear.

Impatiens Busy Lizzie
Hha, ○/◑/●, Hg/Tr/Wb
Known to container gardeners everywhere, and new varieties are introduced every year. Consult a current seed catalogue for colours, compactness, and variations such as doubles. The New Guinea Hybrid type (mainly grown from cuttings) have a more upright habit and usually multi-coloured leaves.
USES Use the New Guinea Hybrids in windowboxes and troughs, the more compact types are grown primarily for flowers in containers of all kinds.
GROWING TIP Will tolerate poor light, but is more compact in good light.

Indian shot, see *Canna*

Ipomoea rubro-caerulea Morning glory
Hha, Cl, ○, Tr/Tu
Also known as *I. violacea* and *I. tricolor*. Large blue or red flowers on thin twining stems. Height: 2.4 m (8 ft).
USE Decorative climber up trellis or wigwam of canes in tub.
GROWING TIPS Deadhead regularly. Grow in a sheltered position.

Iris
Bu, ○/◑, Tr/Wb
The bulbous species most often grown are *I. danfordiae* (yellow, fragrant) and *I. reticulata* (shades of blue and purple). Spring. Height: 15 cm (6 in).
USES Part of a planting of mixed bulbs or in front of dwarf shrubs.
GROWING TIP May split into smaller bulbs that take time to flower again.

Iris stylosa, see *I. unguicularis*

Iris unguicularis Algerian iris
Hb, Ev, ○, Tu/Ur
Also sold as *I. stylosa*. Succession of blue flowers in winter. Height: 23 cm (9 in).
USE Winter-interest containers, alone or with other plants.
GROWING TIPS Best grown near a sunny wall. Needs well-drained compost.

Ivy, see *Hedera*

Japanese maple, see *Acer palmatum*

Jasminum nudiflorum Winter jasmine
Sb/Cl, ○/◑/●, Tu
Succession of small yellow flowers all winter. Height: 2.4 m (8 ft).
USES Grow against a wall for winter interest, or train around a door.
GROWING TIP Needs a trellis or other support.

Juniperus horizontalis ‘Glauca’, see
Conifers

Juniperus × media ‘Blaauw’ and ‘Mint Julep’, see **Conifers**

Juniperus squamata ‘Blue Star’, see
Conifers

Kale, ornamental, see *Brassica oleracea*

Kochia tricophylla Burning bush
Hha, ○/◑, Tr/Tu
Feathery foliage; conifer-shaped plant. Autumn colour. Height: 60 cm (2 ft).
USE Contrast and focal point plant in mixed bedding arrangement.
GROWING TIP Grow in large containers where they have plenty of space.

Lady fern, see Ferns

Lady’s mantle, see *Alchemilla mollis*

Lantana camara
Sb, Pr, Ev, ○, Hg/Wb
Rounded clusters of orange, red, pink, yellow flowers. Height: 45 cm (1½ ft).
USES Good for a mixed basket or for single-subject windowboxes.
GROWING TIPS Overwinter in frost-free place. Can be trained as a standard.

Lathyrus odoratus Sweet pea
Ha, Cl, ○, Tu/Wb
The fragrant sweet pea needs no description. Tall varieties can be grown in a tub or a trough placed against a wall with a trellis, but dwarf kinds are available for a windowbox or tub. Good compact mixtures include ‘Jet Set’ and ‘Knee Hi’, both 90 cm (3 ft).
USE Best for single-subject planting.
GROWING TIP Deadhead continuously to prolong flowering.

Laurus nobilis Bay, sweet bay
Sb, Ev, ○/◑, Tu
A large-leaved shrub ideal for formal shaping. Height: 1.5 m (5 ft).
USES Formal clipped shrub. Can be used to provide bay leaves for kitchen. A pair in matching pots will usually look good flanking the front door.
GROWING TIPS Choose a sheltered position. Protect in winter in cold areas.

Lavandula Lavender
Sb, Ev, ○, Tr/Tu
Aromatic grey or green foliage, blue or purple flowers. Height: 60 cm (2 ft).
USES As part of permanent shrub group, or single-subject planting in a tub.
GROWING TIP Trim over after flowering to maintain a good shape.

Lavender, see *Lavandula*

Lenten rose, see *Helleborus orientalis*

Lobelia cardinalis and L. Fulgens
Hb, Pr, ○/◑, Tr/Tu
Long spikes of bright red flowers and reddish foliage. Height: 60 cm (2 ft).
USES Focal point to add height in planting of mixed summer annuals.
GROWING TIP Store roots in a cold frame or cool greenhouse or light shed.

Houttuynia cordata 'Chameleon'.

Lobelia erinus
Hha, ○/◐, Hg/Tr/Wb
The common blue lobelia with its masses of tiny flowers is available as upright and trailing forms, in shades of pink, red and white as well as blue.
USES Edging for a windowbox or in a hanging basket (especially trailers).
GROWING TIP Never let compost dry out if you want it to keep flowering.

Love-in-a-mist, see _Nigella damascena_

Love-lies-bleeding, see _Amaranthus caudatus_

Lysimachia nummularia Creeping Jenny
Hb, Ev, ○/◐, Hg/Ur/Wb
Trailer with small, rounded leaves (yellow in 'Aurea'). Yellow flowers.
USES Will cascade over edge of windowbox or trail from a basket or urn.
GROWING TIP Compost must be kept moist.

Mahonia 'Charity'
Sb, Ev, ○/◐/●, Tu
Large, spiny leaves. Bold sprays of yellow flowers in winter. Height: 1.8 m (6 ft).
USES Good focal point on patio, and by front door when in flower.
GROWING TIP Enrich compost with extra organic material.

Malcolmia maritima Virginian stock
Ha, ○, Tr/Tu
Masses of small red, lilac, rose or white fragrant flowers. Height: 23 cm (9 in).
USES Quick, cheap colour around base of trees and shrubs, or on their own.
GROWING TIP Allow to self-seed if you want more plants next year.

Male fern, see Ferns

Malus Flowering crab
Te, ○, Tu
White or pink blossom in spring. Some varieties have decorative crab apples in autumn. Two good ones for containers are _M. floribunda_ and _M. sargentii_.

USE Specimen plant in tub.
GROWING TIP Reduce side growths by two-thirds in autumn if necessary.

Maple, Japanese, see _Acer palmatum_

Marguerite, see _Chrysanthemum frutescens_

Matricaria eximia
Hha, ○/◐, Wb
Small white or yellow flowers on compact plants. Height: 23 cm (9 in).
USE Fillers towards the front of a mixed windowbox.
GROWING TIP Grows well in pots, so pot up some spares to fill gaps.

Matteuccia struthiopteris, see Ferns

Mexican orange blossom, see _Choisya ternata_

Milium effusum aureum Bowles' golden grass
Gr, ○/◐, Tr/Tu
Pretty golden grass. Height: 45 cm (1½ ft).

USE Contrast plant in mixed permanent planting.
GROWING TIP If it becomes too tall, just trim it to a suitable height.

Mimulus
Hha, ○/◑, Hg/Wb
Open trumpet flowers in shades of yellow and orange. Height: 30 cm (12 in).
USE Best for single-subject planting.
GROWING TIPS Keep very moist. Deadhead regularly.

Mock orange, see *Philadelphus*

Morning glory, see *Ipomoea rubro-caerulea*

Muscari armeniacum Grape hyacinth
Bu, ○/◑, Tr/Tu/Wb
Spikes of tightly clustered blue flowers in spring. Height: 23 cm (9 in).
USES Good in mixed spring bulb arrangements. Plant around base of trees.
GROWING TIP Will quickly form bold clumps if left undisturbed.

Myosotis Forget-me-not
Bi, ○/◑/●, Tr/Tu/Wb
Masses of small blue (or pink or white) flowers in spring. Height: 23 cm (9 in)
USE As a filler plant around the base of tall bulbs.
GROWING TIP Lift soon after flowering to avoid self-sown seedlings.

Narcissus Daffodil
Bu, ○/◑, Tr/Tu/Wb
The large yellow daffodils need no introduction, but choose some of the dwarfer kinds for windowboxes (and for troughs where wind is a problem). Good ones for containers include 'February Gold', 'Hawera', 'Peeping Tom', 'Tête-à-Tête', and *N. triandrus albus* – this one is only 10 cm (4 in) tall.
USES Compact varieties for windowboxes, taller ones for tubs and troughs.
GROWING TIP Plant so that they grow through lower-growing plants.

Nasturtium, see *Tropaeolum majus*

Nerine bowdenii
Bu, ○/◑, Tu
Long-lasting spidery-looking pink flowers in autumn. Height: 60 cm (2 ft).

USE Makes a focal point when most other flowers have finished.
GROWING TIP Protect container in winter, in cold areas take in for winter.

Nerium oleander Oleander
Sb, Pr, Ev, ○, Tu
White, pink or red flowers against dark green foliage. Height: 1.5 m (5 ft).
USE To create an Mediterranean atmosphere on a patio.
GROWING TIP Move into a conservatory or cool greenhouse for the winter.

New Zealand flax, see *Phormium*

Nicotiana Ornamental tobacco plant
Hha, ○/◑, Tu/Tr/Wb
Trumpet-shaped flowers in shades of red, pink, yellow, green and white. Some do not open during the day; those that do may be less fragrant.
USES Tall, night-flowering type in tub for fragrance. Compact day-opening type with upward-facing flowers in troughs or boxes, integrated or alone.

Nigella damascena Love-in-a-mist
Ha, ○, Tr
Blue, pink, mauve, red flowers like cornflowers. Height: 30 cm (12 in).
USE A cheap and cheerful choice for a single-subject trough.
GROWING TIP Sow directly into the container in spring.

Nolana 'Shooting Star'
Hha, ○, Hg
Pale blue flowers on tumbling stems. Compact foliage.
USES Mixed or single-subject hanging baskets.
GROWING TIP Turn basket regularly to ensure even growth.

Oleander, see *Nerium oleander*

Onion, ornamental, see *Allium*

Ophiopogon
Hb, Ev, ○/◑, Tr/Wb
Perennials with grass-like foliage. *O. jaburan* 'Variegatus' has white-striped leaves, *O. planiscapus nigrescens* is purple-black. Height: 23 cm (9 in).
USE Use for foliage effect in a permanently planted container.

GROWING TIP Avoid a very exposed position in winter.

Pachysandra terminalis 'Variegata'
Sb, Ev, ◑/●, Tu
Creeping evergreen with pretty white and green foliage. Height: 30 cm (12 in).
USE A 'texture' plant to use around base of tree or shrub.
GROWING TIP Divide and replant when they become overcrowded.

Pampas grass, see *Cortaderia selloana 'Pumila'*

Pansy, see *Viola × wittrockiana*

Pelargonium Bedding geranium
Sb, Pr, ○/◑, Hg/Tr/Tu/Ur/Wb
One of the 'essential' container plants. A wide range of colours, flower forms and plant sizes is available. All can be used alone or as part of a mixed planting in troughs and windowboxes. The upright forms of zonal pelargoniums are best in tubs. Ivy-leaved geraniums are popular for hanging baskets because of their trailing habit, but the Continental Cascade type are especially good for single-subject planting. Plant this type close together and do not over-feed otherwise they will produce lots of leaves and not many flowers.
USES As described above.
GROWING TIP Take cuttings in early autumn and overwinter indoors.

Pernettya mucronata
Sb, Ev, ○/◑, Tu
Grown primarily for red, white, pink berries in autumn (grow male and female plants together to ensure a good crop). Height: 75 cm (2½ ft).
USES Grow for autumn and winter interest. Berries last a long time.
GROWING TIP Must have lime-free soil – grow in an ericaceous compost.

Petunia
Hha, ○/◑, Hg/Tr/Wb
The trumpet-shaped flowers of the petunia are a familiar sight in containers of all kinds. The variation in colour, size of flower, flower form, and even habit, is considerable. New varieties appear every year, so consult seed catalogues for inspiration. For baskets try those

described as having a cascading habit.
USE Usually grown with other bedding
plants, but good on their own.
GROWING TIPS Deadhead and feed well
to keep them blooming.

Philadelphus Mock orange
Sb, ○/◑, Tu
Single or double white flowers in summer.
'Belle Etoile' is a good one for a container.
Height: 1.5 m (5 ft).
USE Summer fragrance on the patio.
GROWING TIP Thin out old wood after
flowering.

Phormium New Zealand flax
Sb, Pr, Ev, ○, Tu
Strap-like leaves, some brightly coloured.
Height: 60–150 cm (2–5 ft).
USE Focal point plant in ornate tub.
GROWING TIP Protect whole plant in
winter. May be killed in cold areas.

Phygelius aquaelis
Hb, Ev, ○/◑, Tr/Tu
Orange-buff or yellow tubular flowers
into autumn. Height: 60 cm (2 ft).
USES Good for late colour in permanently
planted trough.
GROWING TIP May be cut back in a hard
winter, but usually regrows.

Pink, see *Dianthus*

**Plumbago, hardy, see *Ceratostigma
willmottianum***

Polyanthus, see *Primula*

Pot marigold, see *Calendula*

Primrose, see *Primula*

Primula
Bi, ○/◑/●, Tr/Wb
The primulas most widely used for
container gardening are polyanthus and
cultivated primroses. Both are available in
a wide range of colours, often with
contrasting eyes, and flower in spring.
Primroses have flowers nestling among
the foliage and are only 15 cm (6 in) tall,
polyanthus flowers are on long stalks
23 cm (9 in) high.
USE Seasonal spring displays, especially in
association with bulbs.
GROWING TIP Although perennials, they
are best treated as biennials.

Prunus 'Amanogawa' Flagpole cherry
Te, ○/◑, Tu
Pink cherry-blossom flowers in spring.
Narrow growth. Height: 2.4 m (8 ft).
USE Flowering tub on a patio where space
is limited.
GROWING TIP Pruning should be
unnecessary.

Pyrethrum
Hha, ○/◑, Tr/Wb
Two foliage pyrethrums are useful for
containers: *P.* 'Golden Ball', 10 cm (4 in)
makes a neat ball of yellow foliage, while
P. ptarmicaeflorum, 30 cm (12 in) has finely
cut silvery leaves.
USE For texture and colour contrast
among mixed summer bedding plants.
GROWING TIP Pinch back
P. ptarmicaeflorum if it becomes too tall.

Pyrus salicifolia 'Pendula' Weeping
willow-leaved pear
Te, ○/◑, Tu
Weeping tree with silvery foliage.
Height: 2.4 m (8 ft).
USE Focal point plant, useful as a contrast
to vivid summer colours.
GROWING TIP May need staking
initially.

Rhododendron
Sb, Ev, ○/◑, Tu
Rhododendrons and azaleas come in many
shapes, sizes and colours, and most flower
in spring or early summer. Consult
specialist catalogues to find suitable
varieties that you like. Look especially for
the Yakushimanum hybrids, which are
very good in containers, but even large
rhododendrons such as 'Pink Pearl' can be
grown successfully.
USE Best as specimen plants on their own.
GROWING TIP They dislike lime; grow in
an ericaceous compost.

Rhus typhina Stag's-horn sumach
Te, ○/◑, Tu
Tree or shrub with very large leaves that
colour strikingly in autumn.
USE Focal point plant for a patio in a large
tub or half-barrel.
GROWING TIPS Prune to tree or shrub
form. Remove suckers if necessary.

Ricinus communis Castor oil plant
Hha, ○, Tu
Large, colourful leaves, often purple or
bronze. Height: 1–1.2 m (3–4 ft).
USE Great for creating a tropical or exotic
effect for the patio at little cost.
GROWING TIP Keep the poisonous seeds
away from children.

Robinia pseudoacacia 'Frisia' Golden
false acacia
Te, ○, Tu
Bright golden foliage that retains its
colour well all summer. Height: 2.4 m
(8 ft).
USE Outstanding as a focal point plant in
a town garden.
GROWING TIP Prune shape and size if it
begins to become too large.

Rosa
Sb, ○, Tu
Roses are not ideal container plants, but
the miniatures can be used in a
windowbox, compact floribunda types
often described as 'patio roses' can be
grown in tubs. A half-barrel will make a
happy home for a climber if positioned
against a suitable wall or trellis.
USE Mainly grown by rose-lovers who
lack a better place to grow them.
GROWING TIP Remember to prune as
you would normal roses.

Rose, see *Rosa*

Salix caprea 'Pendula' Kilmarnock
willow
Te, ○, Tu
Small weeping tree with silvery catkins in
spring. Height: 1.2 m (4 ft).
USES Ideal for producing height on a
small patio, and for spring interest.
GROWING TIP Height depends on how
high the main leader is trained.

Salvia splendens
Hha, ○/◑, Tr/Wb
Spikes of vivid red flowers (other colours
are available). Height: 23 cm (9 in).
USE Usually added to mixed
arrangements for a vivid splash of red.
GROWING TIP To make bushy plants
pinch out growing tip while young.

Sanvitalia procumbens Creeping zinnia
Hha, ○, Hg/Ur
Prostrate plant with masses of small yellow flowers. Height: 20 cm (8 in).
USES Plant as an edging in an urn, or grow solo in a hanging basket.
GROWING TIP Deadhead.

Scilla siberica
Bu, ○/◑, Tr/Wb
Nodding blue bell-shaped flowers in spring. Height: 10 cm (4 in).
USE Very effective as part of seasonal spring display in a windowbox.
GROWING TIP Pot some up to fill in gaps in other containers in spring.

Senecio bicolor, see *Cineraria maritima*

Senecio 'Sunshine'
Sb, Ev, ○/◑, Tu
Grey felted leaves; yellow daisy-type flowers in summer. Height: 90 cm (3 ft).
USE Grow solo. Is also a good contrast to the bright colours of summer flowers.
GROWING TIP If you want the best foliage effect, do not let the plant flower.

Siberian wallflower, see *Cheiranthus × allionii*

Skimmia japonica
Sb, Ev, ◑/●, Tr/Tu
Grown mainly for red autumn berries if a female variety. 'Rubella' is a male but has red buds in winter opening to pink in spring. Height: 75 cm (2½ ft).
USE Autumn and winter interest in a mixed shrub planting.
GROWING TIPS Best in an ericaceous compost. Avoid a very windy position.

Snowdrop, see *Galanthus*

Snowy mespilus, see *Amelanchier*

Spotted laurel, see *Aucuba japonica*

Stag's-horn sumach, see *Rhus typhina*

Sternbergia lutea
Bu, ○/◑, Tr/Wb
Yellow, crocus-like flowers in early and mid autumn. Height: 10 cm (4 in).
USE Autumn interest in front of shrubs in a permanent planting.

GROWING TIP Best left undisturbed to become well established.

Sweet bay, see *Laurus nobilis*

Sweet pea, see *Lathyrus odoratus*

Sweet William, see *Dianthus barbatus*

Tagetes erecta African marigold
Hha, ○/◑, Tr/Wb
Large, globular orange or yellow flowers. Choose compact varieties, to 30 cm (12 in), for containers.
USES Can be mixed with other bedding, but often best planted alone.
GROWING TIP Remove the dead heads, which spoil the effect.

Tagetes patula French marigold
Hha, ○/◑, Hg/Tr/Wb
Yellow, orange or red flowers over a long period. Many forms (including single and double), with new varieties every year. Height: 15–25 cm (6–10 in).
USES Mix with other flowers, or use as edging to a formal windowbox.
GROWING TIP Deadhead.

Taxus baccata 'Fastigiata Robusta', see Conifers

Thrift, see *Armeria maritima*

Thuja occidentalis 'Rheingold', see Conifers

Thuja orientalis 'Aurea Nana', see Conifers

Thunbergia alata Black-eyed Susan
Hha/Cl, ○/◑, Hg/Wb
Yellow, orange or white flowers with or without black eyes. Will climb or trail to about 1.2 m (4 ft).
USES As a trailer in a mixed basket, as climber or trailer in windowbox.
GROWING TIP Provide a small trellis if you want it to climb.

Tobacco plant, see *Nicotiana*

Trachycarpus fortunei Chusan palm, fan palm
Te, Ev, ○/◑, Tu
Unbranched palm with large fan-like leaves. Height: 1.8 m (6 ft).
USE Ideal for creating a tropical effect on a patio.

GROWING TIP Surprisingly hardy, but in cold areas take indoors for winter.

Tropaeolum canariense Canary creeper
Ha/Cl, ○/◑, Tr/Tu
Yellow, fringed flowers. Also sold as *T. peregrinum*. Height: 1.8 m (6 ft).
USE Summer cover for a trellis.
GROWING TIP Watch out for leaf miner and caterpillars.

Tropaeolum majus Nasturtium
Ha, ○/◑, Hg/Tr/Wb
The bright yellow, orange and red nasturtium is well known, but there are many varieties. The variegated 'Alaska' is especially good because the foliage is attractive too. Height of compact kinds: 30 cm (12 in).
USES Use trailers to cascade from baskets, compact kinds in windowboxes and troughs. Nasturtiums may swamp other plants and are often best solo.
GROWING TIP Try to prevent blackfly and caterpillars becoming established.

Tropaeolum peregrinum, see *Tropaeolum canariense*

Tulip, see *Tulipa*

Tulipa Tulip
Bu, ○/◑, Tu/Tr/Wb
Tulips need no description, but the dwarf species tulips and their hybrids are often better than the larger types.
USES Compact varieties are suitable for troughs and windowboxes. Use taller ones in tubs but plant forget-me-nots between them to provide support and mask the long stems.
GROWING TIP Best to plant fresh bulbs each year for containers.

Verbena
Hha, ○/◑, Hg/Ur/Wb
Heads of small but pretty flowers in many colours and shades. Most are seed-raised, but some trailing varieties, such as 'Cleopatra' and 'The Cardinal' are treated as tender perennials and propagated vegetatively.
USE Trailing types make excellent hanging basket plants.
GROWING TIP Take cuttings of perennial types to overwinter frost-free.

Verbena *'Sissinghurst Pink'*.

Viburnum tinus Laurustinus
Sb, Ev, ○/◑, Tu
Clusters of white or pink flowers all
winter. Neat growth. Height: 1.8 m
(6 ft).
USES Can be shaped into an attractive
formal shrub. Good winter interest.
GROWING TIP Shape after flowering if
necessary.

Viola × wittrockiana Pansy
Bi/Hha, ○/◑/●, Hg/Tr/Wb
The pansy is grown in almost every
garden. Although perennial it is almost
always grown as a hardy biennial or half-
hardy annual. By choosing sowing times
and varieties it can be seen in flower every
month of the year. Consult seed
catalogues for suitable varieties.

'Universal' is a particularly popular type
for winter flowering but there are others.
USES Grow as a filler plant among spring
or summer bedding, or on their own. A
ball of pansies grown in a hanging basket
looks good.
GROWING TIP Deadhead regularly to
sustain flowering.

Virginian stock, see *Malcolmia*
maritima

Willow, Kilmarnock, see *Salix*
caprea 'Pendula'

Willow-leaved pear, see *Pyrus*
salicifolia 'Pendula'

Winter aconite, see *Eranthis*
hyemalis

Winter jasmine, see *Jasminum*
nudiflorum

Wintersweet, see *Chimonanthus*
praecox

Witch hazel, see *Hamamelis mollis*

Yucca
Sb, Ev, ○/◑, Tu
Bold sword-like foliage, spikes of huge
white bell flowers in mid and late
summer. *Y. filamentosa* is a popular
species, and 'Variegata' is edged with
cream and yellow margins. Height: 90 cm
(3 ft).
USE Good for making a dramatic
statement on the patio.
GROWING TIP Remove dead flower
spikes and old leaves.

Index

Common names and their Latin counterparts will be found in the A–Z section (pp. 111–128). Main entries on the majority of plants mentioned in the book will be found in this A–Z section which has not been indexed here. Page numbers in *italics* indicate an illustration.